IN SIGHT

GREAT BREAKS

LAKE DISTRICT

◎ Walking Eye App

Your Insight Guide purchase includes a free download of the destination's corresponding eBook. It is available now from the free Walking Eye container app in the App Store and Google Play. Simply download the Walking Eye container app to access the eBook dedicated to your purchased book. The app also features free information on local events taking place and activities you can enjoy during your stay, with the option to book them. In addition, premium content for a wide range of other destinations is available to purchase in-app.

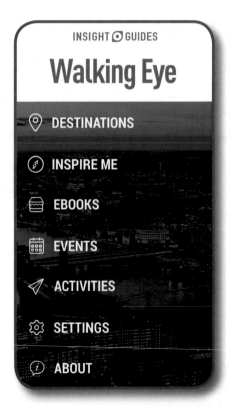

HOW TO DOWNLOAD THE WALKING EYE APP

Available on purchase of this guide only.

1. Visit our website: www.insightguides.com/walkingeye
2. Download the Walking Eye container app to your smartphone (this will give you access to your free eBook and the ability to purchase other products)
3. Select the scanning module in the Walking Eye container app
4. Scan the QR Code on this page – you will be asked to enter a verification word from the book as proof of purchase
5. Download your free eBook* for travel information on the go

* Other destination apps and eBooks are available for purchase separately or are free with the purchase of the Insight Guide book

Contents

Travel Tips

Lake District's Top 10

There's water and Wordsworth everywhere – but there's still much more to drink in. Here are just some of the high spots of this beautiful corner of Britain

▲ **Dove Cottage.** Imagine William Wordsworth and his wife and sister cramped in this former Grasmere pub, reciting poetry. See page 59.

▲ **Aira Force.** This graceful tumble of water is spanned by a picturesque stone bridge. See page 31.

▲ **Derwent Water.** Climb aboard a classic boat on one of the most beautiful of all the lakes, dotted with islands, surrounded by magnificent mountains and close to the market town of Keswick. See page 67.

▶ **Langdale Valley.** A perfect mountain valley, its green floor and fell-sides rising to the bare rock of Langdale Pikes, and at its head the great bulk of Bow Fell. See page 88.

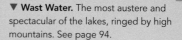

▼ **Wast Water.** The most austere and spectacular of the lakes, ringed by high mountains. See page 94.

▲ **Furness Abbey.** Extending along the lovely Vale of Deadly Nightshade are the splendid red sandstone remnants of a once powerful Cistercian community. See page 104.

▼ **Tarn Hows.** A real piece of peace, this Lakeland icon is set in dense woodland interlaced with paths and created by the merging of three tarns. See page 47.

▲ **Beatrix Potter sites.** Meet Mrs Tiggy-Winkle in Hawkshead, and visit Hill Top, home of her creator, the talented Beatrix Potter. See page 49.

▼ **Windermere.** Cumbria's longest stretch of water is the ideal leisure lake. On its eastern bank is the fun-loving town of Bowness, from where you can take cruises on the lake, or visit the World of Beatrix Potter. See page 21.

▲ **Castlerigg.** This ancient stone circle from the mists of time shows how humankind has always been in awe of nature. See page 55.

Langdale Valley.

Overview

An Extra-special Place

Well loved, well walked and wildly romantic, the Lake District is one of the best-known corners of Britain. Yet for all its fame, there is always something here to discover

The Lake District is among the most romantic places in the world – indeed this is where the 18th-century Romantic Movement began. The high, green fells and rocky, sometimes snowy summits falling steeply into deep, still waters, have a dream-like, timeless quality. Whether driving or walking, visitors feel drawn into their wild embrace. Over every hill, round every bend, landscapes shift and turn, diving into narrow, stream-filled valleys, opening up into vistas.

These small mountains (only four of them more than 3,000ft/900m) are not hard to conquer, yet they can be wild and treacherous. And the normally tranquil lakes, some so deep nobody knows what lies on their fathomless beds, can cut up rough, too.

The bare slopes and summits are the result of the grazing of the Herdwick sheep. Fellsides and whitewashed farms on rock ledges sit in fields closed off by dry-stone walls. Life is hard here: look at the old quarries and mines.

Atlantic Ocean

North Sea

NORTHERN IRELAND

IRELAND

Lake District

GREAT BRITAIN

London

FRANCE

Red deer, red squirrels and ospreys make their homes here. Wild daffodils, stars of the most famous poem by the great Romantic poet, William Wordsworth, flourish in meadows and in the deciduous woods.

The Poet Laureate of the Lakes inspired the first tourists, and today tourism is paramount for the local economy. Yet however crowded it gets – more than a quarter of a million visitors might arrive for a Bank Holiday – you will still find peaceful areas.

LANDSCAPE

The Lake District National Park covers an area of 880 sq miles (2,279 sq km), all of it in the county of Cumbria, and is the largest national park in Britain. From Ennerdale in the west to Shap in the east, it stretches 40 miles (64km) wide. Shaped like a giant wheel, its ridges radiate from a hub of high mountains ('fells', from the Norse), separating the valleys ('dales') and a score of big lakes. From Great End, near the heart of the district,

Mediobogdum Roman Fort, Hardknott Pass.

the view north extends over Solway Firth to the blue hills of Scotland. A distant blue-grey smudge in the east is the Pennines. To the west and south is Morecambe Bay.

Windermere, the largest lake, is more than 10 miles (16km) long but relatively narrow. Ullswater, the second in size, has its head among the high fells and its tail in the pastoral landscape around Pooley Bridge. In addition to the big lakes, there are numerous small mountain tarns scooped out by Ice-Age glaciers.

GEOLOGY

Skiddaw slates, the oldest visible rocks, form the friable northern fells, plus that isolated bulk of Black Combe in the southwest. They were laid down more than 500 million years ago in a shallow sea. Some 50 million years later, a volcano erupted to form the Borrowdale volcanics of Central Lakeland. The Silurian slates of the Southern Lakes, composed of shales, slates, grits and flags, are (like the Skiddaw group) metamorphic and sedimentary. A fourth major geological element forms a narrow band of Coniston limestone between the volcanics and the Silurian slates.

The appearance of the Lake District we see today was determined

The nestled town of Coniston.

some 50–60 million years ago, a period of great mountain building that also thrust up the Alps and the Himalayas. In Cumbria, an immense dome was created, into which radial drainage patterns were cut. During the last Ice Age, which ended 10,000 years ago, ice sculpted the fells, and scoured and deepened river valleys into lakes.

CLIMATE

The changing climate is part of the high drama of the Lakes. Bad weather can close in fast, reducing visibility to a minimum, and hikers ignore bad weather warnings at their peril.

The fells form a natural barrier to weather fronts that sweep in from the Irish Sea in the west. Moisture-laden air rising over the fells forms clouds and accounts for the region's heavy rainfall. Seathwaite, in Borrowdale, is actually the wettest inhabited place in England, with approximately 124in (315cm) of rain a year.

On dull days there are generally breaks in the cloud, through which sunlight streams, bringing sections of the landscape into sharp relief. Snow falls between December and Easter, and, while there is no permanent cover, pockets may linger in deep gullies until

England's largest natural lake, Windermere is some 220ft (67m) deep.

Going Green

With increased funding in 2015 to various local government agencies, the 'See More: Cumbria and the Lake District' project will continue to provide initiatives to encourage people to make fewer car journeys. There will be more bus routes and dedicated bus tours, increased steamer trips, 60 new free guided bike rides, and electric cars and bikes to hire. Be aware that bus routes and timetables can change (see page 120).

Mountain Goat, a service that links in with local buses and ferries.

midsummer. Most valleys are quite low lying, and a dale might remain green when flanking fells are gleaming white.

FARMING

Five thousand years have elapsed since humankind made its first mark on the landscape. Celts, Romans and Angles cleared away tracts of the old forest that extended up the hills as far as 2,000ft (600m). Around AD 925, Norse settlers from Scandinavia adjusted their lifestyle to the high hills, on which they summered their cattle and sheep. From them come the many local words, such as beck (stream), gill (gorge) and thwaite (clearing).

When Norman lords granted the monastic orders large tracts of the

Lake District in the 11th century, these became a range for sheep bred from the native 'crag' sheep. Known as Herdwicks, an old English word for a monastic pasturage, the name is used to this day for the nimble animal that has a face white as hoarfrost, a coarse fleece, which is dark at first, becoming greyer with age, and four solid legs to enable it to cope with the mountainous grazing.

Farming is the basic industry of Lakeland. The farms have stocks of sheep and a few beef cattle. Tending the sheep gives plenty of work for well-trained curs or collies, which respond to the whistles of the farmer with barks – vital here when flushing sheep from among rocks or dense areas of bracken.

A hazard for drivers: sheep can appear on the road around any bend.

Guide to Coloured Boxes

Eating
Fact
Green
Kids
Shopping
View

This guide is dotted with coloured boxes providing additional practical and cultural information to make the most of your visit. Here is a guide to the coding system.

Food and Drink

Traditionally, the role of food in the Lakes was to provide plenty of calories for the hard labour of farming and mining, so there is a legacy of hearty recipes that are perfect after a day of tramping across the fells. Breakfast would generally have consisted of very thick **poddish** (porridge), and, working on the principle that 'it's your stomach 'at 'ods your back up', there was a wide range of cakes and breads to keep you going throughout the day. However, perhaps the most iconic of Lakeland recipes is the **tatie pot**, a stew of mutton or lamb, black pudding and potatoes, often served at local festivities.

The availability of excellent traditional ingredients has underpinned something of a foodie revolution in recent years, with talented young chefs taking an interest in local foodstuffs. A great resource on food in Cumbria is www.artisan-food.com, with links to, and reviews of, local producers.

MEAT

The native Herdwick sheep produces some of the best **lamb** and **mutton** in Britain, perhaps due to its diet of heather and berries. An unusual local delicacy from the sheep is **Herdwick ham**. Usually 'ham' refers to pork, but this is a leg of mutton cured in brine and spices and then smoked. The 'ham' is eaten raw and goes well with fruit preserves, especially pickled damsons (see box).

Another local speciality, **Cumberland sausage**, is made from fresh pork and produced in a large herby coil (it is easily recognisable, as it is not divided up into links). Traditionally it includes good lumps of fat within to help with the cooking. It has become one of EU's protected regional foods, which means it must be produced, processed and prepared in Cumbria with a meat content of no less than 80 percent.

Cumberland also has a long tradition of curing pork hams, and the unsmoked, slightly salty local product can be excellent.

FISH

As you might imagine in a region of lakes, freshwater fish such as trout and salmon figure highly on menus. However, the real Lakeland delicacy is the **Windermere char** (a saltwater fish left behind after the last Ice Age). Catches of the fish, which tastes a little like trout, are now strictly controlled, and it is no longer commercially available. Howver, it is still fished for using traditional methods between July and

Cumbria is renowned for the quality of its pork – do try to sample some sausages or pork pies.

Lyth Valley Damsons

These small, rather tart plums with their purple skins are delicious, especially when made into jam or steeped in gin. September is the best time to tour the Lyth Valley (southeast of Bowness), where they are grown. Road-side stalls and local shops usually have a good supply, though some years fruit is scarce. See the website of the Westmorland Damson Association at www.lythdamsons.org.uk for more information.

Damson blossom is a great attraction in Lyth Valley in spring.

October, so you might just find it on the table at a local restaurant. When it is cooked, it is either grilled or potted (preserved with spices and butter).

Another preserved fishy delicacy of the region is the **potted shrimps** from Morecambe Bay, preserved in butter like the char. The centre of the shrimp industry is Flookburgh not far from Grange-over-Sands. They are usually served with a slice of lemon and thin rounds of toast.

CAKES AND SWEETS

Cumbria has some wonderful traditional cakes. In Grasmere don't miss out on the famous **gingerbread** (see page 59). The ginger that goes into this used to be brought in through Cumbria's ports, and imports of other spices, and especially rum, found their way into other local specialities. These include **Cumberland rum nicky**, a tart filled with a mixture of rum, dates and ginger, **Kendal pepper cake**, a spicy fruitcake, and **Cumberland rum butter** (also known as 'hard sauce'), a mixture of butter, rum, nutmeg and sugar.

For afternoon tea you might encounter sweet yeast breads such as **Borrowdale tea bread** and **Hawk-shead wigs**. However, the sweetest product of the Lakes is **Kendal Mint Cake**, which finds its way into every many a hiker's rucksack.

ALE

The main drink of the Lake District, apart from its famously pure water, is **ale**. The largest local brewery is Jennings, which has been producing beer in Cockermouth since 1874. A number of microbreweries have started up in the Lakes producing fine local ales, often served in the pubs to which they are attached. Look out for beer from the Barngates Brewery in Ambleside, the Keswick Brewing Company, the Hawkshead Brewery, the Coniston Brewery, and the Unsworth Yard Brewery in Cartmel.

Find our recommended restaurants at the end of each tour. Below is a Price Guide to help you make your choice.

Eating Out Price Guide

Two-course meal for one person, including a glass of wine.

£££ = over £35
££ = £20–35
£ = under £20

Kendal Castle, home of the Parrs.

Tour 1

Kendal to Windermere

This 30-mile (48km) journey takes you through the pretty landscape of the southern Lake District, from the town of Kendal to Windermere on the shores of its largest lake

Southeast Lakeland lacks the high drama of Central Lakeland, but its quieter hills offer many rewards, and though this tour could be done in a day, there is plenty of scope for walking and staying longer.

Kendal, the market centre for the region, is known as the 'auld grey town' not because it's dull and boring, but because of the colour of limestone with which it is built. A lively place with hiking gear shops and Vacancy signs on many of its front windows, this is the main centre of the southern Lakes and provides a place from which to start your exploration.

A tranquil contrast with urban Kendal can be found in picturesque Kentmere. This valley is a cul-de-sac but hill-walkers can carry on up Kentmere

Highlights

- Abbot Hall Art Gallery
- Museum of Lakeland Life & Industry
- Kendal Museum
- Kentmere
- Bowness Bay and the 'Steamers'
- The World of Beatrix Potter
- Blackwell
- The Lyth Valley

Pike (2,397ft/730m) and then on to the long, straight ridge of High Street (2,719ft/829m), which once carried the Roman road between the forts at Ambleside and Penrith.

The destination on this route is Windermere, England's largest lake. The old steamers (now running on

Kendal Mint Cake – not actually a cake.

and named after the owners of the houses that stood at their end. Some good examples remain, with plaques explaining their history, and are worth exploring. Notice, too, in Stricklandgate a stone-built house with a protruding sign of a hog with bristles, originally made when the premises were used by a maker of brushes.

The town was the birthplace of Henry VIII's sixth and last wife, Catherine Parr. Her family occupied **Kendal Castle**, now a ruin on a small hill overlooking the town.

Catherine's prayer book is on display, and can be seen on request, in the **Town Hall**, which was rebuilt on a grand scale with a clock tower in 1825. An outdoor market is still held every Wednesday and Saturday around the old **Market Place**; there is also an indoor market here (Mon–Sat).

Kendal is perhaps best known outside the Lake District as the home of **mint cake**, first made here in 1869.

diesel) ply the lake and take the visitor to within sight of the rock turrets of the Langdale Pikes. Bowness Bay, which the children's author Arthur Ransome (see page 41) referred to as Rio, has a fascinating waterfront and the country's finest collection of steamboats. The return to Kendal is through the Lyth Valley, back in limestone country. The limestone gives a special flavour to the fruit of a profusion of damson trees, which are white with blossom in May and laden with fruit in September and October.

KENDAL

Kendal ❶ lies just outside the Lake District National Park. It is easily reached by train, changing at Oxenholme (4 mins away) on the main line between Glasgow and London.

The settlement dates back to the 8th century and owed its later prosperity to the wool trade, which transformed the town. By the 18th century there were around 150 'yards', little alleys often containing workshops

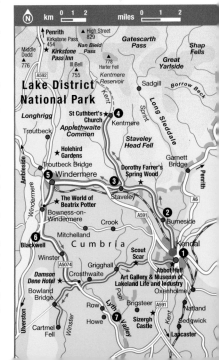

This bar of mint-flavoured sugar, widely used by walkers and climbers for an energy boost, was famously used on the first successful ascent of Everest in 1953.

Riverside and museums

A broad, traffic-free riverside path west of the River Kent leads to the **Abbot Hall Art Gallery** (www.abbothall. org.uk; Mon–Sat Mar–Oct 10.30am– 5pm (also Sun July–Aug noon–4pm), Nov–Feb 10.30am–4pm). This distinguished 18th-century building has an outstanding collection of fine art. The works are shown on a rotation basis and include pieces by John Ruskin, painters from the St Ives School, and a fine collection of canvases by the 18th-century portrait painter George Romney, who had his first studio in Kendal, and who died here. There is a particularly interesting display of landscape watercolours from the 18th and 19th centuries, when the Romantic landscape of the region captured the imagination of artists Edward Lear and

Kendal, a lively commercial centre, is a good base for exploring the southern Lakes.

J.M.W. Turner, whose watercolour of *Windermere* can be seen here. The gallery also holds temporary exhibitions.

Beside the gallery is the **Museum of Lakeland Life & Industry** (www.lakelandmuseum.org.uk; Mon–Sat Apr–Oct 10.30am–5pm

Abbot Hall Art Gallery has many watercolours by 18th- and 19th-century artists inspired by the Lakes, including J.M.W. Turner.

and a good display on the local Arts and Crafts Movement. The museum occasionally holds events at which you can see local craftworkers making traditional artefacts (see the website for details).

The **Kendal Museum** (www.kendalmuseum.org.uk; Tue–Sat 10am–4pm), near the railway station, has imaginative displays relating to local archaeology and natural history, including a section of items associated with Alfred Wainwright (see page 113), the extraordinary Lakeland guide book writer, including a number of his fine illustrations. There are also spectacular examples of rocks and minerals from local mines collected by potholer John Hamer.

Wool merchants' endowments enriched Holy Trinity Church.

(also Sun July–Aug noon–4pm), Nov–Mar 10.30am–4pm). Using a series of re-created rooms, including a farmhouse kitchen and living room, the museum seeks to evoke the domestic and working lives of the people of the area before modern communications opened up the Lakes to the outside world. There are two rooms devoted to the life and work of Arthur Ransome, author of *Swallows and Amazons* (see page 41),

Anglicans and Quakers

By Abbot Hall is the **Church of the Holy Trinity**, which began to take shape in the 12th century and continued until it reached a grand scale through the wealth of the wool merchants who endowed it. One of the aisles is named after the Flemish weavers who were brought in to help the town become prosperous.

The first impression on entering the building is one of vast size; the church

Fields of Kendal Green

Kendal's motto – *Pannus mihi pani*, 'wool is my bread' – reflects its former importance as a wool-making town. William Camden, writing in 1582, saw the 'tenter fields', where cloth was stretched out to dry after being dyed, and compared the sight with 'vine orchards in Spain'. Kendal Green was the most famous colour, made by mixing woad (blue) with dyer's yellow broom. One of the customers is said to have been Robin Hood.

Sheep made Kendal a wealthy wool-manufacturing town.

The Brewery Arts Centre hosts special exhibitions every year as part of the Kendal Mountain Festival.

is 103ft (31m) wide, making it one of the broadest naves in the country. Displayed on the north wall is a helmet, said to have belonged to 'Robin the Devil', the nickname of Colonel

1657 Chocolate House

This chocolatier and café can be found at 54 Branthwaite Brow, Kendal. Despite its name, the building dates from the 1630s, and the staff wear costumes of the time, offering handmade pralines, truffles and cakes (Mon–Sat 9.30am–5pm; www.chocolatehouse1657.co.uk).

Chocoholics rejoice!

Huddleston Philipson, who rode his horse into church during divine service. He was seeking but did not find Colonel Briggs, one of his Cromwellian adversaries. The church also contains the chapels and tombs of prominent local families, including those of the Parrs.

On Stramongate, not far from the bus station, is a slightly different religious site. In the Friend's Meeting House is the **Quaker Tapestry** (www.quaker-tapestry.co.uk; Apr–mid-Dec Mon–Sat 10am–5pm). This display of 77 hand-embroidered panels tells the story of the Quaker Movement. It took 14 years to complete and is the work of over 4,000 people.

Art and leisure

The **Brewery Arts Centre** (www.breweryarts.co.uk), on Highgate, is an attractive arts complex with a cinema and theatre that often hosts live music. The centre also has a decent restaurant, bar and café and is one of the venues of the annual Kendal Mountain Festival.

Kendal Leisure Centre (www.northcountryleisure.org.uk; Mon–Fri

The weir at Staveley on the River Kent.

STAVELEY

The train continues along the **River Kent** and on to **Staveley** ❸ (there is no direct bus from Burneside, although bus No. 555 runs regularly to Staveley from Kendal bus station). Between the Kent and Gowan, the riverside woodland is brightened in spring by clusters of small wild daffodils.

Dorothy Farrer's Spring Wood, a mile (2km) east of Staveley, is a nature reserve of the Cumbrian Wildlife Trust (www.cumbriawildlifetrust.org. uk), where springtime flora includes bluebell, wild garlic, wood anemone, the rare herb paris and early purple orchid. Many different species of birds can be spotted, including pied and spotted flycatchers, redstarts and willow warblers.

St James's in Staveley, dating from 1865, has a stained-glass east window designed by Edward Burne-Jones.

KENTMERE

From Staveley you can walk (3 miles/ 5km) up to the secluded village of **Kentmere** ❹. The road meanders amiably through a knobbly and well-wooded landscape. The glint

The road to the secluded village of Kentmere.

from 6.30am, Sat–Sun from 8am, closure times vary) is a modern building that incorporates a swimming pool, gym and theatre. The Lakeland Sinfonia (www.lakelandsinfonia.org.uk) put on concerts here throughout the year.

BURNESIDE

On leaving Kendal, take either the bus (No. 45, not Sun) from Stricklandgate, or the train to **Burneside** ❷, where the water of the Kent has been used as power for mills since corn was first ground here in 1283. Burneside Hall, now attached to a farmhouse, has a pele tower (pronounced 'peal'). These square defensive buildings were built in the 14th century to defend against raids by the Scots.

Also in Burneside is the factory of James Cropper, 'Europe's leading coloured and specialist paper manufacturers', which has been in the same family for five generations.

The 84-mile (135km) Dales Way long-distance footpath from Ilkley in West Yorkshire to Bowness passes through Burneside, where the Jolly Anglers pub is a popular watering hole for weary walkers.

Steamer loaded with passengers on Windermere.

of water indicates what remains of **Kentmere Tarn**, which shrank considerably when the valley was drained to reclaim land for agriculture. The road ends about a mile (2km) north of the village, beyond which is a rough track leading to Nan Bield Pass, which connects Kentmere with the Haweswater valley.

St Cuthbert's Church

On a ledge high above the valley, presiding over a scattering of houses and farms, sits **St Cuthbert's Church**. To reach it, amble along the little lanes and cross the tiny bridges, surrounded by an astonishing stonescape. The enormous boulders that lie in the fields around St Cuthbert's Church were borne to their resting places by glacial ice. Others have been incorporated in dry-stone walls, demonstrating as well as anywhere the craftsmen's special skills. Keep bearing right, crossing a bridge over the River Kent and returning to the village on a lane between high walls.

There are great views up the valley of the fells that mark the Borrowdale volcanic zone. Mardale Ill Bell, Yoke and High Street are part of a horse-

shoe of ridges that appeal to tougher fell walkers. A much more gentle stroll from the church is to Kentmere Hall, another building that developed from a simple pele tower that acted as a sanctuary for local families and their livestock. The 15th-century hall, which served as a farmhouse for a long time and is still part of a privately owned farm, can be seen from the road.

St Cuthbert's Church sits amidst a wonderful stonescape.

WINDERMERE AND BOWNESS

Return to Staveley and carry on to **Windermere ❺** (this is the terminus for rail services; bus No. 555 also passes through here). Before the arrival of the railway in 1847 this was the hamlet of Birthwaite, situated a mile (2km) from the lake anciently known as Vinard's Mere. Windermere is very much a Victorian town and owes its growth to the visitors who arrived by train and who had to pass through here to reach the lakeside at Bowness just below the town.

Continue down Lake Road to the main centre of Bowness delightfully situated on Bowness Bay. **Bowness-on-Windermere** is a holiday town, and one in which to enjoy just wandering around. The promenade at **Bowness Bay** has a lively atmosphere, as boats come and go at the various piers, waves lap against shingle, gulls squawk and the majority of swans seem to spend most of the day out of the water, waddling about begging for food. The 'steamers' – *Swan*, *Teal* and *Tern* – are operated by Windermere Lake Cruises (timetables and prices can be found on their website, www. windermere-lakecruises.co.uk). Services run across the lake and between Lakeside, Brockhole, Bowness and Waterhead (for Ambleside). Check the website for special offers on fares.

Soaking up the atmosphere

The most historic building in Bowness, **St Martin's Church**, has an east window that consists of 15th-century glass said to have been brought from Cartmel Priory (see page 100). **Belsfield**, at one time home of the Furness industrialist H.W. Schneider, is now a hotel. Schneider's iron-hulled boat, *Esperance*, which was a

Fit folk will cycle the 10 miles (16km) from Windermere to Kendal.

Steamers waiting for their load of visitors at Bowness Pier, with the Victorian Belsfield Hotel behind.

model for the houseboat that makes an appearance in Arthur Ransome's *Swallows and Amazons*, is part of the Windermere Steamboat Collection. It was displayed at the Windermere Steamboat Museum until its closure in 2006. Along with other Lakeland boats from this important collection, it will be housed in the striking new complex, **Windermere Jetty**, due to open in 2017, (www.windermere jetty.org for details). Boats held by the collection include *Margaret*, the oldest yacht in Britain dating from 1780, and *Dolly*, which is the world's oldest mechanically powered boat. Launched in 1850, it sank nine years later, and was recovered in 1962. Visitors will be able to view yachts, ferry boats, rowing boats and canoes, plus motor boats from the 1920s to 1950s.

Occupying a central position at Bowness, and a great favourite with children, is **The World of Beatrix**

High Fells Viewpoint

For a magnificent view of Windermere, head for Biskey Howe, which is reached by following the steep Helm Road (just off Queen's Square in Bowness) and then heading left. From here you can see the whole extent of the lake, from north to south. In clear weather many of the nearby high fells, including those of the Langdale Pikes, are visible from this viewpoint and are pointed out on a stone plaque.

Head for Biskey Howe to get the best views of the lake.

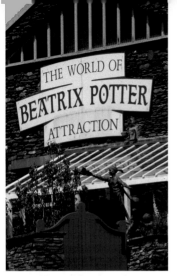

Peter Rabbit and friends can be seen at The World of Beatrix Potter.

Potter (www.hop-skip-jump.com; daily Apr–Sept 10am–5.30pm, Oct–Mar 10am–4.30pm). The exhibition starts with a four-minute film that introduces all the books and takes you through a series of re-created scenes populated by characters such as Peter Rabbit, who has an outdoor garden, Benjamin Bunny and Mrs Tiggy-Winkle. There is a Potter-themed tearoom with tables indoors and on the garden terrace. The attraction's website also describes a 13-mile (21km) walk around sites associated with the writer's life and work.

BLACKWELL

To return to Kendal, you can either take the train or bus No. 555 back the way you have just come or, if you have your own transport (it is about a 10-mile/16km bicycle ride with some steepish hills), you can carry on in a loop via Crosthwaite and over Scout Scar. Currently, there is no bus along this route.

From Bowness, just opposite the church, follow the signposted turning

for **Blackwell** ❻ (www.blackwell. org.uk; daily Mar–Oct 10.30am–5pm, Nov–Feb 10.30am–4pm), the Arts and Crafts house designed by M.H. Baillie Scott for a wealthy Manchester brewery owner. Built between 1897 and 1900, Baillie Scott's experiment in light, space and texture is unique in retaining almost all of its original decoration and has been sympathetically renovated. The house is furnished with items by leading Arts and Crafts designers, such as William Morris, and the tiled fireplaces are particularly attractive. The tearoom terrace in the garden has lovely views over the surrounding countryside.

LYTH VALLEY

Following the A5074 you can head up through the **Lyth Valley** ❼, *lyth* being a Norse word referring to the long slope leading up to the limestone plateau of Whitbarrow. Although it has

Blackwell, a particularly well-restored Arts and Crafts house built for a Manchester Brewer.

Tour I

Lyth Valley

Daffodils in St Anthony's churchyard, Cartmel Fell.

an A classification, the road is relaxing to drive here and offers long views over Windermere.

A few minutes further south, in a countryside of little fields and scattered homes, lies **Winster**, with a much-photographed, white-walled old post office in a house dated 1600. Its environs are full of flowers in summer. Just beyond Winster, the name of a hotel, **Damson Dene**, draws attention

Sheep taking it easy in a field above the Lyth Valley.

to a famous product of the Lyth Valley, the damsons, which have a nutty flavour. Ripe by September, some are eaten immediately, others are preserved as jam and yet more go to make gin. In May it's worth driving down the valley and back again to see the glory of damson blossom, which in a good year gives an impression of a light fall of snow.

CARTMEL FELL

Near Damson Dene, a road heading right leads to Bowland Bridge. Continue up the hill beyond the bridge, where a signpost indicates **Cartmel Fell St Anthony's Church**. In summer, the church is tucked away behind a screen of leaves. The building dates back to the early 16th century, when it was a chapel-of-ease in the parish of Cartmel, a village about 7 miles (11km) away. The furnishings include a three-level pulpit and fascinating pews, one (for Cowmire Hall) seemingly fashioned from the old chancel screen.

CROSTHWAITE AND SCOUT SCAR

Return to **Damson Dene** and take the road that goes as straight as an arrow to **Crosthwaite** ('clearing where a cross was raised') on the northern side of the Lyth Valley. There is no Lyth Beck, just two little rivers, one called Pool and the other Gilpin. This part of the Lake District is in delightful contrast with the austere fell country further to the north and west. There are small fields, lots of trees and some hedges as well as the traditional dry-stone walls.

Follow the signs for Kendal on an unclassified but well-surfaced road. The road climbs over **Scout Scar**, the name Scout coming from the Norse skuti, meaning a steep cliff. The name is accurate: Scout Scar has a fearsome series of limestone crags and an almost level ridge walk extending south for well over a mile (2km). At the summit there are views over Morecambe Bay and across to the Central Lakes.

Turn aside on foot and follow a path along part of Scout Scar to a **mountain indicator** nicknamed 'The Mushroom' because of its distinctive roof.

The road then leads down the steep hill from Scout Scar all the way back to Kendal.

Eating Out

Kendal
The Grainstore and Warehouse Café
Brewery Arts Centre, Highgate; tel: 01539-725133; www.breweryarts. co.uk; restaurant Mon–Fri 5–9pm, Sat–Sun noon– 9.30pm; café Mon–Sat 9am–5.30pm.
You'll find excellent tapas and pizza in the Grainstore and local pies, homemade soups and sandwiches in the café. £

Meeting House Café
Friends Meeting House, Stramongate; tel: 01539-722975; www.quaker-tapestry.co.uk; Mon–Sat 10am–4pm.
This is one of the best places for vegetarian and vegan food in the Lakes, with light meals and fabulous cakes and puds. £

Windermere and Bowness
Gilpin Hotel
Crook Road; tel: 015394-88818; www.thegilpin.co.uk; daily all day.
The restaurant at this luxury retreat is great for afternoon tea, while the five-course evening menu highlights modern English cuisine. £££ (tea £)

Hooked
Ellerthwaite Square; tel: 015394-48443; www.hookedwindermere. co.uk; Tue–Sat dinner only, closed Dec–Jan.

There's seafood delight on a plate at Hooked, where the produce is locally sourced and skilfully cooked, enhanced by Mediterranean and Asian flavouring. ££

The Lighthouse
Main Road; tel: 015394-88260; www.lighthouserestaurant windermere.co.uk; daily 8.30am–late.
Come to this three-floored bistro-style restaurant for breakfast, lunch, afternoon tea, cocktails or dinner. Tastes of the Mediterranean are a speciality. ££ (dinner)

Miller Howe
Rayrigg Road; tel: 015394-42536; www.millerhowe.com; daily breakfast, lunch and dinner.
With Lancashire cheese, Cumbrian beef and Herdwick mutton, this is a great place to try some well-cooked and imaginative local food. £££

Crosthwaite
The Punch Bowl
Lyth Valley; tel: 015395-68237; www.the-punchbowl.co.uk; daily 8.30am–late.
The dishes at this lovely old inn, such as roast loin of cod, Cumbrian rump of lamb, and confit of pork belly, are delicious, and the wine list is excellent. ££

Hartsop cottage.

Tour 2

Ullswater and Kirkstone Pass

Starting from Penrith, this 52-mile (84km) tour takes you along one of the most spectacular valleys in the Lakes, over the high Kirkstone Pass and down into Ambleside

The great expanse of Ullswater stretches from craggy volcanic fells to an altogether softer landscape resting on friable Skiddaw slate. The fells assembled around the upper reach appear to leap straight from the water, like mountains from a Norwegian fjord. There was once a passion, on the part of those with taste and leisure, to shatter the silence and listen to the echoes. The Duke of Portland mounted some brass guns on a boat for this very purpose.

Unlike other lakes, Ullswater has two pronounced bends, giving a dogleg shape. The name is Norse, meaning Ulfr's lake — although which Ulfr gave his name to the lake is hard to say, as the name was common among the Norse settlers.

Highlights

- St Andrew's Church, Penrith
- Aira Force
- Helvellyn
- The Kirkstone Pass
- Townend
- Holehird Gardens
- Lake District Visitor Centre, Brockhole
- The Armitt, Ambleside
- Dalemain

The road south out from the lake goes through the 1,489ft (454m) Kirkstone Pass, which takes its name from a large pointed rock, said to resemble a kirk or church. The road is kept open throughout the winter when some other high Lakeland passes are blocked by snow, an increasingly rare occurrence in recent years. On the tour described here, the Kirkstone is crossed twice, the second time being from south to north, when the views across the fells are most dramatic.

PENRITH

The route starts with the town of **Penrith ❶**. This is easily reached on the main railway line from London to Glasgow, and is only about 15 mins from Carlisle or 25 mins from Oxenholme. The town has about it a ruddy tinge from red sandstone, of which it is built and after which it is probably named – 'red hill' in ancient Cumbric.

Penrith is a pleasant market town, and its food shops and restaurants show the wealth of local produce. Pick up a leaflet on town trails to find out where William and Dorothy Wordsworth went to school and other highlights of its long history.

The town began as a settlement associated with the Roman forts of Vireda and Brocavum and during the Middle Ages was the capital of Cumbria. As in many places around the Lakes local industry was dominated by the wool trade, and Penrith was a great weaving centre. It has been a market town since the 13th century, with a number of open squares making up the town's centre, and a market is still held every Tuesday. The main (Market) square has an attractive clock tower, built in 1861.

Penrith's 14th-century **Castle** (daily Apr–Oct summer 7.30am–9pm, Nov–Mar 7.30am–4.30pm; free) is a picturesque ruin, of which only the walls survive. These, and the now grassed-over moat, are set in a park near the railway station. The castle was once the home of Richard, Duke of Gloucester, who subsequently became King Richard III of England.

Sparrowhawks come to the Lakes in spring.

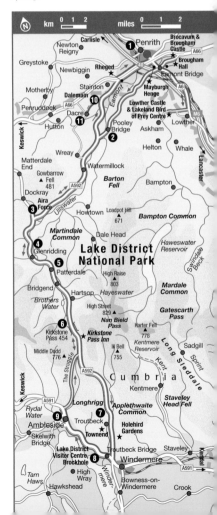

The town's other important monument is the Georgian **St Andrew's Church**. Redesigned by Nicholas Hawksmoor, much of St Andrew's dates from 1722, although it retains its 13th-century bell tower. In the churchyard you'll see two upright stones flanking a trough known as the **Giant's Grave**. This is said to be the resting place of Owen Caesarius, king of Cumbria AD920–37. The 10th-century **Giant's Thumb**, a Norse Cross, is also associated with Owen. It is thought that he erected it in memory of his father.

Penrith Museum (www.eden.gov. uk/museum; Mon–Sat 10am–5pm, also Sun Apr–Oct 11am–4pm; free) is located in the centre of town on Middlegate in the old Robinson's School, founded in 1670. It has displays on local geology and archaeology, including finds from the local Roman forts.

Also in the town is the **Penrith Playhouse** on Auction Mart Lane, home to the Penrith Players theatre company, which stages productions throughout the year.

Around Penrith

The Romans had an important fort (Brocavum) at Brougham, a mile or so down the road towards Appleby (bus 563 leaves Penrith Bus Station for Appleby about every two/three hours; not Sun). Before you reach the fort you will come to the impressive ruined walls and keep of **Brougham Castle** (Apr–Sept daily 10am–6pm; Oct 10am–4pm, Nov–Mar Sat–Sun 10am–4pm). This is the former home of the Clifford family but was initially built in the 13th century by a follower of King John.

South of Penrith is the Estate of the Lowthers, Earls of Lonsdale, whose family name was bestowed on the River Lowther. Their ruined **castle** has now undergone heavy restoration (www.lowthercastle.org; daily 10am–5pm), and in its grounds is the

Lakeland Bird of Prey Centre (tel: 01931-712746; Apr–Oct daily 11am–5pm). This has a large number of birds of prey, including hawks, eagles, buzzards, owls and falcons, and they are flown daily (starting at 2pm, weather permitting). There is also a tearoom and small gift shop.

To Pooley Bridge

From Penrith bus station take bus No. 508 towards Patterdale. The bus runs daily from Easter until late October and

Bikes on the camper van: a classic Lakeland jaunt.

Pooley Bridge, where Ullswater spills over into the River Eamont.

from Mon–Sat during the winter. There are more services during the summer school holidays and weekends.

Just south of Penrith you will pass through the small village of Eamont Bridge where the remains of two stone circles can be seen. The larger, **Mayburgh Henge**, retains a single standing stone, and nearby is **King Arthur's Round Table**, a circular earthwork with a fanciful name. Both date back to around 2000 BC.

Also in Eamont Bridge you'll find the 14th-century **Brougham Hall** (www. broughamhall.co.uk; daily dawn–dusk, workshops: 10am–5pm; free). The hall, which is subject to ongoing but discreet renovation work, is home to an array of Arts and Crafts workshops. Its heyday was during the 19th and early 20th centuries, when it was known as the 'Windsor of the North'. It received numerous royal visits and reputedly held some riotous parties.

Landscape Language

Place names record the history and heritage of the county. Celtic, Norse, Irish and Norman have all been great influences. Old English 'pike', as in Langdale Pikes (from *pic*), means a peak or sharp summit. Stickle comes from *sticele* or *stikill*, a steep place. The local term for lake is 'watter' or 'mere' – hence Wastwater and Windermere. Only one stretch of water has 'lake' in its title, and that is Bassenthwaite Lake, to the north of Keswick.

The Langdale Pikes.

The Tourist Information Centre at Glenridding has details of walks and activities around Ullswater, the second largest of the lakes.

The bus carries on to the small village of **Pooley Bridge ❷**, which has a backdrop of wooded Dunmallet (*dun* indicating a hill fort). Pooley Bridge lies at the northern end of Ullswater, where the fast-flowing River Eamont, a tributary of the Eden, leaves the lake. An alternative way on from here might be by boat as this is one of the stops for the Ullswater Steamers (see page 31). Otherwise the bus will continue on to Glenridding and Patterdale.

Aira Force, the best-known waterfall in the Lakes.

ULLSWATER

The lake of **Ullswater**, almost 8 miles (13km) long, has a sinuous appearance and a setting that gets progressively grander with the passing miles. It was on the shore of this lake that William and Dorothy Wordsworth saw the 'dancing' daffodils. Dorothy jotted in her journal her impressions and placed the spot 'beyond Gowbarrow Park' (presumably to the south of the junction where a road heads north to Dockray). She wrote: 'They grew among the mossy stones about and about them; some rested their heads upon these stones as on a pillow for weariness; and the rest tossed and reeled and danced, and seemed as if they verily laughed with the wind…' William later adapted her prose as a poem, *Daffodils*, with the memorable opening line: 'I wandered lonely as a cloud…'

The Raven, one of the four historic Ullswater steamers.

Continue on the A592; just by the turn-off for Dockray is **Aira Force** ❸, a spectacular waterfall now in the care of the National Trust. The falls are reached after following a good path that climbs steadily for about a quarter of a mile (0.5km). If you are lucky, you may spot a red squirrel among the trees as you climb. The slender waterfall tumbles a total of 65ft (20m) in a gorge flanked by trees and crossed by a small stone bridge. The Force has occasionally frozen, becoming an impressive icicle.

Gowbarrow Fell

This 1,578ft (481m) fell, once a deer park, is a good place on which to wander, at relatively low elevation, to take advantage of its grand views of Ullswater. For this 4-mile (6.5km) walk, start up Gowbarrow by going northwards from the Aira Force car park, then bear left to the ruins of a shooting lodge. After reaching the summit, continue on to the valley of Aira Beck and return via the popular footpath used by visitors to the falls.

Glenridding

Goldrill Beck, the main feeder for the lake, flows from Brothers Water and enters Ullswater not far from **Glenridding** ❹. The name is said to mean 'glen overgrown with bracken', and for three centuries the village was a busy lead mining centre. But since the Greenside mines closed in 1962, the area has been landscaped, and Glenridding is now entirely given over to tourism. A bridleway links up with a footpath extending to the summit of **Helvellyn** (3,116ft/ 950m), the third-highest peak in the Lake District.

Ladies of the Lake

Glenridding is the main base for the **Ullswater Steamers** (the boats sail all year, see www.ullswater-steamers. co.uk for detailed information on fares and timetables; tel: 017864-82229). There are five historic boats in the fleet: *Raven*; *Lady of the Lake* (the oldest working passenger vessel in the world, built in 1877); *Lady Wakefield*; *Western Belle*; and the smaller, originally seagoing, vessel, *Lady Dorothy*, which continues the service during the winter months. One-way tickets are ideal for walkers who wish to spend some time exploring the valley.

Gowbarrow Fell is not a great height, but the views are wonderful.

Patterdale **5**, between Glenridding and Brothers Water, is the name of both a village and valley, a favourite of walkers, and especially favoured by Alfred Wainwright. It gives its name to the Patterdale Fell Terrier dog, and it is supposed to be connected with St Patrick. Indeed, a local legend has it that the Irish saint took refuge here after being shipwrecked on Duddon Sands in AD 540.

Bus 508 stops in Patterdale and then carries on to Hartsop en route for Bowness via the Kirkstone Pass. This extended route is a seasonal service only running daily from Easter until late October. Check for days and times on www.cumbria.gov.uk/buses.

HARTSOP

Dovedale, a tributary valley, ends on the shores of **Brothers Water**, an expanse of water less than half a mile (0.8km) long and a quarter of a mile (0.4km) wide. The name was formerly Broad Water, but romance invests it with the sad tale of two brothers who drowned, when ice broke beneath them. This area is owned by the Na-

Dancing daffodils beside Ullswater inspired Dorothy and William Wordsworth to wax lyrical.

tional Trust but leased to a local farmer. From a car park near the outflow of the lake there is a pleasant walk to the vicinity of **Hartsop Hall**, a 16th-century Grade I listed house and an important example of a working valley head farm. It has many fascinating features, such as priest holes, which the farm-

Like a number of Cumbrian villages, the 17th-century grey stone houses in Hartsop had spinning galleries to make woollen cloth.

er will show you if you ask him nicely (www.hartsophallcottages.com).

On the opposite side of the main road, the village of **Hartsop**, with 17th-century buildings, reclines in a cul-de-sac. A track continues into the Hayeswater Valley, under the massive bulk of High Street. *Hartsop* means 'valley of the hart': red deer from the 'forest' at Martindale are often seen in the area. Hartsop has a workaday farm and some dwellings with 'spinning galleries', where, it is said, spinsters spun wool from the fell sheep.

KIRKSTONE PASS

At the southern end of Ullswater the road heads towards Windermere, reaching 1,489ft (454m) at **Kirkstone Pass ❻**, and rises through some spectacular scenery, though the crossing can be dreary in wet or misty weather. Near the summit is **Kirkstone Pass Inn**, which has evolved from a late 15th-century building. The thick-walled, heavy-roofed building looks across to the face of Red Screes. Above the screes is the 2,541ft (774m) fell of Middle Dodd, and if you want to stretch your legs here, a path from opposite the inn leads up above the screes to the summit.

Kirkstone Pass, the high point between Ullswater and Windermere.

TROUTBECK

On the way down towards Windermere on the A592, try to stop off at **Troutbeck ❼**, a village with a fascinating assembly of 17th- and 18th-century buildings. The **Mortal Man** is an inn with a sign relating to an especially strong ale: Thou mortal man, who liv'st

Helvellyn by Striding Edge

This is one of the finest days out on the fells, but you will need to be properly equipped and have a good head for heights. Take the footpath from either Glenridding or Patterdale that climbs up to Hole-in-the-Wall above Bleaberry Crag. From here the narrow ridge of Striding Edge climbs up to the summit of Helvellyn. To complete the horseshoe, carry on down the less daunting Swirral Edge and Catsycam to the north.

Helvellyn needs proper equipment and a head for heights.

A Canadian canoe race passing by Brockhole.

by bread, What is it makes thy nose so red? Thou silly fool, that look'st so pale, 'Tis drinking Sally Birkett's ale. **Troutbeck Church**, surrounded by a pretty graveyard, is chiefly famous for its large east window. This was the work of a trio of artists: Edward Burne-Jones, William Morris and Ford Maddox Brown. Morris was assisted by the others when they were on a Lake District fishing holiday. Ann Macbeth, who lived locally from 1921 until 1948, adorned the building with splendid tapestries. Several roadside wells in Troutbeck are dedicated to saints.

At the southern end of the village, and appropriately named **Townend**, is a superb house cared for by the National Trust (mid-Mar–Oct Wed–Sun, guided tours at 11am and noon, general admission 1–5pm; garden 11am–5pm). Townend was built in stone and slate during the 17th century and lived in by the Browne family, generations of whom filled it with an array of exquisitely carved wooden furnishings and a collection of more than 1,500 books. The displays of domestic tools and period costumes are particularly interesting.

HOLEHIRD

Just after Troutbeck, on the left-hand side of the road, look out for a sign relating to **Holehird**. The house is now a nursing home and is not open to the public, but the gardens are maintained by the Lakeland Horticultural Society and are now one of the area's top attractions (www.holehirdgardens.org.uk; daily dawn–dusk, reception desk Apr–Oct 10am–5pm; free). The grounds are beautifully maintained by volunteers, and the flora includes a wide range of alpine and

Townend, now cared for by the National Trust.

rockery plants. The gardens are also home to the national collections of Astilbes, Hydrangeas and Polystichum ferns (for more information, see Plant Heritage at www.nccpg.com).

BROCKHOLE

If using public transport, the No. 508 bus will drop you off at Bowness Pier, from where you can catch bus 599 to Ambleside (more frequent in summer, check for times). Otherwise turn right on the A591 to **Troutbeck Bridge** and, along a stretch of road flanked by mature beech trees, fol-

low signs for the **Lake District Visitor Centre, Brockhole** ❽ (www. brockhole.co.uk; house, café and shop; daily 10am–6pm; café closes at 5.45pm; free, charge for car park and some attractions). The grounds (daily dawn–dusk), with their superb views of Windermere and the Langdale Pikes, were designed by Thomas Mawson in 1898. Attractions include formal gardens, scented and kitchen gardens, and a wildflower meadow. There are opportunities for activities both on water and land, plus a treetop aerial 'adventure' (booking advised).

The house at Brockhole has displays and exhibitions on the region's history, geology and wildlife, plus lots of interactives and fun for children. There is also a gift shop and a café with terrace.

AMBLESIDE

The town of **Ambleside** ❾ has been described as the hub of the wheel of beauty. Roads radiate into the central valleys, and Windermere Lake Cruises (see page 21) operate from Waterhead Pier, a mile (1.5km) away. Although it dates back to Roman times, when they built the fort of Galava (see page 43) close to the lake, Ambleside is a mainly Victorian

---

Endangered Fish

The schelly (*Coregonus stigmaticus*) is a very rare fish only found in the deepest parts of Ullswater and three other nearby bodies of water: Brothers Water a little up the valley, Red Tarn below Helvellyn and Haweswater, where they are preyed on by cormorants, which as a result are being culled. Resembling, and often called, a 'freshwater herring', the fish are on the IUCN Red List of Threatened Species.

With endanged species such as schelly, fishing needs to be controlled.

town of splendid slate buildings erected by local craftsmen. The Ambleside campus of the University of Cumbria is on the north side of the town.

The spired Victorian **church** has a mural relating to a local custom, the Rushbearing, which takes place in July (see page 65). An earlier building is the diminutive **Bridge House**, beside Rydal Road. Built in 1723, it rests on a bridge over Stock Beck and administered by the National Trust. Higher up the beck is an old **corn mill** with a waterwheel. Market day is Wednesday, when stalls are set up in King Street.

Museums and culture

Ambleside is home to the amazing collections of **The Armitt** (www.armitt.com; museum: daily 10am–5pm; www.armitt.com), an art gallery, museum and library. It was founded by Mary Armitt, who set up a library in 1909 with books from the collections of Wordsworth and Ruskin. The collections quickly grew, with artefacts from the excavations at Gala-

va fort and watercolours donated by Beatrix Potter. Today the museum has displays of books and paintings, geology and archaeology, as well as local social history.

The main cultural centre in Ambleside is the award-winning **Zeffirellis** on Compston Road (www.zeffirellis.com). Its independent cinema shows a good mix of Hollywood and arthouse films, there are regular performances of live music in the upstairs jazz bar, and there is also a good restaurant.

One of the joys of Ambleside is its independent shops. You'll find everything for your outdoor needs from walking boots to mountain bikes. There's plenty of choice, too, of gifts, artworks and books.

THE STRUGGLE

If you have your own transport you can return to the Kirkstone Pass from Ambleside via the steep road known appropriately as **The Struggle**. This starts near the church and opposite

Bridge House in Ambleside is now an information centre.

If you go on a long, arduous walk, it's a good idea to use poles.

the large car park on Rydal Road and crawls up a steep gradient to the Kirk-stone Pass Inn – be aware that this is a very tough climb on a bike. Look out for the views northward from the pass, which are magnificent. Soaring fellsides, littered with boulders, frame a picture of Brothers Water and the high fells east of Patterdale.

If you plan to return to Penrith on public transport, take bus 599 to Windermere and then the 508 bus for Penrith (or by train, change at Oxenholme).

Dalemain

If returning via Pooley Bridge and Ulls-water, just to the west of the A592 is the Grade I-listed **Dalemain** ❿ (www.dalemain.com; Easter–Oct Sun–Thu 11.45am–4pm, closes 3pm in Oct; guided tour at 11.15am). The house can also be reached by an easy 1-mile (1.5km) walk from the village of **Stainton**, which is on the X4 and

Dalemain Apples

Over 100 old-fashioned roses and numerous 18th-century named-variety apple trees perfume the gardens at Dalemain. Apple soup is one of the seasonal dishes served in the tearoom, which is set in the mansion's medieval hall.

Often used in historical films, Dalemain is a place for apple soup.

Make sure to take some waterproof and windproof jackets with you.

X5 bus route from Penrith. Dalemain has been the home of the Hasell family since 1679 and is really three houses in one: it is Georgian in outward appearance, the facade hides an Elizabethan house, and at the core of the building is a Norman pele tower. One of the most impressive rooms is the Medieval Hall, now the location of a tearoom serving good cakes and lunches. A herd of fallow deer occupies a walled park behind the house.

DACRE

From Dalmain, an estate road is a pleasant 1-mile (1.5km) walk to the village of **Dacre** ⓫. The church here is believed to have been the site of Dacore, a monastery mentioned in Anglian times by the Venerable Bede, who relates that a young man whose eyelid was swelling at a fearful rate had it touched with a lock of the hair of St Cuthbert and within a few hours had been cured. **Dacre Castle** (not open to the public) dates from the mid-14th century. It became the property of the Hasell family in 1723 and was then restored. A further restoration took place in the 1960s, when it became the home of Bunty Kinsman. Her amusing account of life at Dacre Castle was published in 1971 under the title *Pawn Takes Castle*.

St Andrew's church

St Andrew's in Dacre, based on a 10th-century Viking grave monument, is the place to go bear hunting. In the corners of the graveyard are stone effigies known as the **bears**, which may have adorned the castle, or possibly marked the corner boundaries of a much older burial ground. The stones are much eroded and some believe that they represent lions, not bears. There are clear views of Dacre Castle from the churchyard.

Go bear hunting in Dacre churchyard to find the castle's escapees.

RHEGHED

From Dacre continue on the A592 to reach **Rheged – The Village in the Hill** (www.rheged.com). Europe's largest grass-covered building is named after Cumbria's Celtic Kingdom. There is a cinema, play areas, exhibitions, cookery school, shops and places to eat. The same company owns the award-winning amenities at **Tebay Services** (www.westmorland.com) on the M6 (between Jn 38 and 39). The farm shop here sells an excellent selection of local produce.

Return to Penrith on the A66 or, if travelling by bus, hop on the X4 or X5 from Rheged car park back to Penrith.

The entrance to Rheghed, a grassed-over complex designed to resemble a Lakeland fell.

Eating Out

Penrith
Rheged Centre
Redhills; tel: 01768 868 002; www.rheged.com; daily 8.30am–5pm, times vary.
This complex has three excellent eateries: a food-bar, a café and the Peter Sidwell @ Rheged Café. All serve wholesome local food. £

Troutbeck
The Mortal Man
Guy Lane; tel: 015394-33193; www.themortalman.co.uk; daily lunch and dinner.
This pub has a great menu of local food, including smoked haddock chowder and venison steak. ££

Ambleside
The Drunken Duck
Barnsgates; tel: 015394-36347; http://drunkenduck.co.uk; daily lunch and dinner.
Well known for its delicious own-brewed ales, the Duck also serves imaginative dishes based on local produce. ££
The Old Stamp House
Church Street; tel: 015394-32775; www.oldstamphouse.com; Wed–Sat lunch and dinner, also Tue lunch.
Chef Ryan Blackburn uses Cumbrian produce to create fabulous dishes at this restaurant opened in 2014 to great acclaim. £££
The Priest Hole
Church Street; tel: 015394-33332; www.thepriesthole.co.uk; daily lunch and dinner.
Set in a great old building, this restaurant dishes up tasty modern British food and traditional favourites. ££
Rothay Manor
Rothay Bridge; tel: 015394-33605; www.rothaymanor.co.uk; daily breakfast, lunch and dinner.
An upmarket country-house hotel with excellent afternoon teas, set Sunday lunches and top-class dinners. £££
Zeffirellis
Compston Road; tel: 015394-33845; www.zeffirellis.com; daily 10am–10pm.
The vegetarian pizzeria here has, as you would expect, good pizza, and a decent range of antipasti and pasta dishes, all at a very reasonable price. £

Literary Lakes

When Wordsworth wanted to be inspired, he simply went for a walk. Other poets have found the Lakes a spur to creativity, while its nature has produced classic children's stories

I t was the fondness of the Romantics for the wild and awe-inspiring landscape of the Lakes that established them on the literary map, none more so than the Wordsworth siblings.

LAKELAND POETS

William and his younger sister Dorothy were born at Cockermouth in 1770 and 1771, 20 months apart. After leaving school they sojourned for a while in the south, returning in 1799 to live in Dove Cottage, Grasmere (see page 59). Dorothy's prose work is best seen in her *Journal*. Apart

from his immense output of verse, including his most famous work, *The Prelude*, William wrote a perceptive guide book to the area.

Wordsworth and the friends who congregated around him – Samuel Taylor Coleridge, Robert Southey and Thomas De Quincey – became known as the Lakeland Poets. Southey, who settled for a while in Keswick, was appointed Poet Laureate in 1813. They in their turn had been inspired by the poet Thomas Gray who visited the area in 1769. His *Journal* is described as one of the first examples of modern travel writing.

Dove Cottage, home of William Wordsworth.

RUSKIN TO RANSOME

The Lake District was the home of the prolific art critic John Ruskin. He lived for 50 years at Brantwood, above Coniston Water (see page 43). After his death in 1900 his assistant, the author W.G. Collingwood, established the Ruskin Museum in Coniston.

Coniston Water was where Arthur Ransome spent his childhood holidays, at Nibthwaite, and they provided the inspiration for his *Swallows and Amazons* adventure books for children. And it was the landscape and animals around her home in Near Sawrey (see page 50), close to Hawkshead, that made Beatrix Potter a children's favourite.

A sense of place

Perhaps more than any other writer, Alfred Wainwright (see page 113) has conveyed the spirit of the Lake District through his beautifully hand-written, hand-drawn books of walks through the fells. They have become a bible for the hiker and find a place in every serious walker's rucksack.

Coniston Water, third
largest of the lakes.

Tour 3

Coniston and Hawkshead

**This 20-mile (32km) tour starts at Ambleside and runs
through the pretty landscape of the southern Lakes, which
inspired the likes of Ruskin, Ransome and Beatrix Potter**

This is a glorious area of gentle hills, lakes and tarns, woodland, white-walled farms and cottages. Before local government was reorganised in 1974, this was all in Lancashire, and those who think of the Red Rose county as being a region of industrial towns with forests of mill chimneys might reflect on this during their journey.

One of the highlights is Tarn Hows, which is frequently portrayed in books and on picture postcards as an example of scenic Lakeland. It has a haunting beauty despite being part man-made. The water is retained by a dam to regulate its flow to the Monk Coniston estate. The trees here, upstart conifers, impart an unexpected resinous smell.

This tour also brings you into contact with some of the Lake District's

Highlights

- Galava
- Coniston Water
- The Ruskin Museum
- Brantwood
- Tarn Hows
- Hawkshead
- The Old Grammar School
- The Beatrix Potter Gallery
- Hill Top

writers: Arthur Ransome based *Swallows and Amazons* on the childhood holidays he spent by Lake Coniston; Beatrix Potter met Peter Rabbit at Near Sawrey; and John Ruskin sat and pondered art and life from his home at Brantwood.

The paths and tracks around Loughrigg Fell offer beautiful views of Langdale Pikes, Helm Crag and Windermere.

Much of this tour as it can be undertaken using a combination of the daily bus No. 505 (the 'Coniston Rambler') from Ambleside and the Cross Lakes Experience bus routes. Bus services between Ambleside and Coniston, the two main centres of southern Lakeland, are regular and reliable. Once you are in Coniston, you can take advantage of the Cross Lakes Experience ticket, a joint venture between the steamers, Mountain Goat services and Stagecoach that you can hop on and off, taking your bike with you. You can download the Cross Lakes Experience brochure on www.mountain-goat.co.uk.

GALAVA

Starting from Ambleside (see page 35), visit the ruins of the Roman fort of **Galava**, by Borran's Park near the head of Windermere. There are no standing structures here, just an expanse of grass with some exposed stones left by the excavations, but information panels help to bring the site

to life. The fort was built in AD 79 and expanded 50 years later.

LOUGHRIGG FELL

To continue, catch bus No. 505 from Kelsick Road. Heading for Coniston from Ambleside, the road runs just to the south of the sprawling, multi-peaked **Loughrigg Fell ❶**. This relatively low hill (1,099ft/335m) makes a rewarding excursion, and at Ambleside's Tourist Office you can obtain leaflets on walks on the fell, from which there are stunning views of Ambleside and Rydal Water.

TO WATERHEAD

The road continues south and winds up and down between areas of woodland. The bus passes through the pretty village of Hawkshead (see page 48), but stay on board for the moment and carry on as the road skirts the bottom of Hill Fell. The road then briefly climbs up a steep hill before descending to **Waterhead ❷** at the head of Coniston Water.

CONISTON WATER

Coniston Water is the third largest of the lakes, 5 miles (8km) long and more than 180ft (55m) deep. Because of its straight length, during the mid-20th century it was considered an

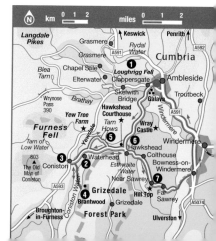

Coniston village is surrounded by fells; the highest of them is the Old Man of Coniston at 2,634ft (803m).

ideal place to try and break the water speed record. This was first attempted here by Malcolm Campbell in 1939, when he reached 141.74mph (228.11kph) in his boat *Bluebird K4*.

The attempts were carried on postwar by his son Donald, who broke the record four times on Coniston Water between 1956–9. His last attempt here in 1967 ended in tragedy, when, in an effort to break the 300mph (483kph) barrier, his boat *Bluebird K7* broke up, and he was killed. Campbell's body, and the wreck of *Bluebird*, were not recovered until 2001. This was carried out by the Bluebird Project (www.bluebirdproject.com), which continues to restore as much as possible of the boat back to its original condition to put on permanent display at the Ruskin Museum (see page xx).

The lake greatly influenced the work of writer and journalist Arthur Ransome. The author belonged to a Leeds family, and the holidays of his boyhood were spent at Nibthwaite, near the outflow of Coniston Water. He was in the Yewdale area on a protracted holiday in 1908 when he came up with the story of *Swallows and Amazons*. His series of books was inspired by memories of boating on Windermere and Coniston Water. The great hill Wetherlam (2,502ft/763m), which dominates the Yewdale valley, appears in both *Swallowdale* and *Pigeon Post*, and one of the Yewdale farms is described in his novel *Winter Holiday*.

Cooling off in the shallows, but do keep to the edge: the lake is 184ft (56m) deep.

Coniston

The bus continues around the lake to the village of **Coniston ❸**. The presiding spirit here is John Ruskin, whose grave at **St Andrew's Church** has a Celtic-style cross of Tilberthwaite stone, with a design (reflecting his many interests) devised by his secretary and good friend, W.G. Collingwood, another writer, who taught Arthur Ransome to sail in his boat, *Swallow*. Also in the graveyard is Donald Campbell, who was buried here after his body was recovered in 2001.

Collingwood and Campbell also share the glory with Ruskin in the **Ruskin Museum**, founded in 1901, one year after the writer's death (www.ruskinmuseum.com; mid-Mar–mid-Nov daily 10am–5.30pm, mid-Nov–mid-Mar Wed–Sun 10.30am–3.30pm). The museum is not far from the church and has excellent displays on the life of Ruskin and details of Campbell's water speed record attempts, as well as local life, history and geology. A specially built wing dedicated to *Bluebird K7* has opened at the museum.

The mountain that presides over the village is **The Old Man of Coniston** (2,634ft/803m). This can be climbed by following the well-marked path from the village, taking you to the summit high above the tarn of Low Water. On the way up you will see many traces of copper mining and quarries for slate.

The Gondola

Ruskin lived across the lake at Brantwood. The best way to reach the house is to take the Victorian steam-yacht **Gondola** that still cruises on Coniston Water to a regular timetable and with a full head of steam.

Quarries and Mines

The Lake District fells hold a variety of minerals that have been exploited for centuries. Copper was mined in various places, notably the Newlands Valley. Graphite, also known as 'wad', was hewn from underground workings near Seathwaite. Granite of various hues comes from quarries at Shap. Iron ore was extracted in Eskdale, and slate has been quarried near Coniston, at Elterwater and near the Kirkstone Pass.

Cumbria produces 'green' slate; this quarry is in Elterwater.

John Ruskin

The writer, artist and critic John Ruskin (1819–1900) was both a social reformer – espousing an early form of Socialism – and one of the prime movers in the Arts and Crafts Movement. He was a great champion of J.M.W. Turner, and his book on Venetian architecture was highly influential. Ruskin's personal life was turbulent, and he famously did not consummate his marriage to Effie Gray, claiming his wife's body was 'disgusting'.

Learn all about the writer at the Ruskin Museum in Coniston.

The *Gondola* sails from Coniston Pier (daily Apr–Oct daily, weather permitting, first sailing 11am). If the weather is chilly, visitors can find shelter in the upholstered first-class saloon. The design for this 1859 steam launch was approved by John Ruskin, a man with demanding tastes. It lay wrecked in Nibthwaite Bay for many years but was rescued by the National Trust and given an extensive restoration. The steam engine, powered by environmentally friendly reconstituted wooden logs, is remarkably responsive and quiet as the craft glides through the water.

If you miss the *Gondola*, or are in Coniston over the winter, another boat service, the Coniston Launch (tel: 017687-75753; www.coniston launch.co.uk; daily Mar–Oct first sailing 10.45am; Nov–Mar, five sailings a day weather permitting), also sails from Coniston Pier to Brantwood and Waterhead. The two wooden boats date from the 1920s and have been converted to run on solar power. A restored boat, *Campbell*, was launched in 2011.

John Ruskin's Brantwood, where he lived for 50 years, is much as he left it, and it has one of the most spectacular views of any house in England.

The Gondola steams through the waters, powered by eco-friendly logs.

BRANTWOOD

John Ruskin lived at **Brantwood** ❹ (www.brantwood.org.uk; mid-Mar–Nov daily 10.30am–5pm, Dec–mid-Mar Wed–Sun 10.30am–4pm) from 1872 until his death in 1900. The house overlooks Coniston Water and the Coniston Fells, giving one of the finest views in England. Brantwood has been preserved much as it was at the time of Ruskin's death and is full of his paintings, furniture and objects that this much-travelled critic and writer collected over his lifetime. The house sits in beautifully landscaped grounds and gardens, some laid out to designs by Ruskin. At the *Brantwood Café* you can have lunch on a lovely terrace.

YEWDALE

To the north of Coniston along the A593 is Yewdale (no bus on this route), which is owned by the National Trust. Wordsworth described the valley as 'level as a Lake'. The 17th-century farms are architecturally outstanding. One of these, **Yew Tree Farm**, to the west of the A593 was once owned by Beatrix Potter, and it is now a guesthouse with luxury accommodation.

TARN HOWS

Bus No. 505 runs from Coniston to Hawkshead. Leaving the bus at Monk Coniston, you can walk the 3.5 miles (5.5km) up and back to the beautiful **Tarn Hows** ❺. A good footpath leads around the tarn, which was created during the 19th century by building a dam and merging three tarns that had lain in marshland. A tarn, incidentally, the Norse for teardrop, is formed by glaciers and not fed by a stream.

Beatrix Potter bought the area around the tarns in 1929; she left it to

Tarn Hows, one of the most photographed spots in the Lakes.

One of the most popular ways to get around – and to see for yourself what attracted so many writers and poets to the Lakes.

the National Trust on her death. The views of Wetherlam and the Langdale Pikes from the southern side of the lake, where the path takes to higher ground, are magnificent. For those only wishing to walk round the tarn (1.8 miles/3km), the Mountain Goat bus 525 links with bus 505 at Hawkshead direct to Tarn Hows.

THE COURTHOUSE

Bus 505 continues towards Hawkshead. Near the junction with the Ambleside road is the **Courthouse** (access only with the key from the National Trust Shop, The Square, Hawkshead). Just a short work across the fields brings you to the distinguished building, all that remains of a range of 15th-century manorial buildings (Hawkshead Hall) associated with Furness Abbey (see page 104).

HAWKSHEAD

Traffic has been all but eliminated from the narrow streets and squares of **Hawkshead** ⑥, adding to the attraction of this wonderful little town, with white-painted buildings, yards and alleys. Originally a Norse pastoral settlement, Hawkshead continued its association with the wool trade during the Middle Ages, when it was part of the lands of Furness Abbey.

St Michael's Church

Dominating the village is St Michael's Church, a large and handsome struc-

St Michael's Church, Hawkshead.

A tumble of foliage on a house in attractive Hawkshead.

Wordsworth's school

One of the most important buildings in Hawkshead is the **Old Grammar School** (www.hawksheadgrammar. org.uk; Apr–Sept Mon–Sat 10am–1pm, 1.30–5pm, Oct Mon–Sat 10am–1pm, 2–3.30pm), founded in 1585 by Archbishop Edwin Sandys. William Wordsworth was a pupil here for seven years, and he carved his initials on his desk. He lodged with Mistress Tyson either at Hawkshead or nearby Colthouse (there were Tysons in both places). The school, with a fine sundial above the entrance, now houses a small museum describing the history of the building and the world of the Hawkshead Grammar School Foundation, which provides grants to young people to assist their further education, vocational training, and entry into work.

Potter's world

Beatrix Potter's spirit broods over several shops in Hawkshead specialising in her books and related souvenirs, and at the National Trust's **Beatrix Potter Gallery** (tel: 015394-36355; daily June–Aug 10.30am–5pm, mid-Feb–mid-Mar Sat–Thu 10.30am–3.30pm, mid-Mar–May, Sept–Oct Sat–Thu 10.30am–5pm; admission by timed ticket at busy times). The gallery oc-

ture indicative of 15th-century prosperity. Its inner walls are adorned with murals and painted texts dating from the 17th century. In the graveyard is a war memorial designed in a Celtic style by W.G. Collingwood. The church holds concerts on several evenings (8pm) in July and August. When viewed from the knoll on which the church is built, the whitewashed houses of the old town below appear to huddle together. Each building is a little different; they are fine examples of Lakeland vernacular architecture.

Beatrix Potter

Beatrix Potter (1866–1943) spent her life surrounded by plants and animals, and she was involved in preserving Herdwick sheep. Her two pet rabbits, Benjamin and Peter, star in her books. She became an authority on mycology (lichens and fungi), illustrating her work with beautiful paintings. Illustrations were an essential part of her later books that told stories about animals, set in the countryside around Hawkshead.

Writer, illustrator and farmer, Potter was wedded to the Lakes.

cupies offices used by Potter's solicitor husband, William Heelis. The interior of the office has been preserved much as it was during his lifetime. There is an annually changing exhibition of original sketches and watercolours painted by the multi-talented Potter, as well as a permanent display on her life.

Esthwaite Water

On the southern outskirts of Hawkshead is a right turn towards Grizedale (see page 108), and heading left will bring you to the hamlet of Colthouse, once part of the Furness Abbey estate.

From Hawkshead, the Mountain Goat bus service will take you on to Near Sawrey and Far Sawrey (Apr–Oct), two clutches of picturesque cottages, tea-rooms and pubs, and Potter's Hill Top home. The route follows **Esthwaite Water** (which means 'lake by the eastern clearing') a 1.5-mile (2km) long lake where the young Wordsworth would skate. The lake has a delightfully pastoral setting and sustains a trout fishery, where you can learn fly-fishing.

NEAR SAWREY

The road from Hawkshead along Esthwaite Water leads to **Near Sawrey** ➐ at the far end of the lake. Beatrix Potter's first Lake District holiday with

The picturesque village of Near Sawrey takes its name from 'sawrayes' meaning a muddy place.

her family was at Wray Castle, a Victorian mock-Gothic edifice near Windermere. She grew so fond of this quiet part of what was then North Lancashire that she used the royalties from her first book, *The Tale of Peter Rabbit*, published in 1900, to purchase **Hill Top** (tel: 015394-36269; Sat–Thu, June–Aug 10am–5.30pm, mid-Feb–Mar 10.30am–3.30pm, Apr–May, Sept–Oct 10am–4.30pm; admission by timed ticket) in Near Sawrey.

Being one of the major attractions of the Lake District, and relatively small, the house can admit only a limited number of visitors at any one time, and in high season there may be queues. Fans of the books will recognise parts of the house and gardens from her il-

Getting their feet wet.

lustrations. When she married William Heelis, they resided in **Castle Cottage** (private) almost directly opposite Hill Top.

From Near Sawrey, the bus continues on to **Far Sawrey** where you can catch the large car-carrying **Windermere Ferry** (check the website www.cumbria.gov.uk for timetable). Guided by metal cables stretched from shore to shore, the journey only takes a few minutes across to Bowness Pier, from where you can take the bus back up to Ambleside.

The Lakes produce some excellent ales – try the local one at the Hawkshead Brewery.

Eating Out

Coniston
The Black Bull
Coppermines Road; tel: 015394-41335; www.blackbullconiston.co.uk; daily, bar: breakfast, lunch and dinner, restaurant: dinner.
The bar and restaurant food at this old inn is definitely above average, and best washed down with one of their own-brewed ales. ££
The Bluebird Café
Lake Road; tel: 015394-41649; www.thebluebirdcafe.co.uk; daily 10am–5pm (seasonal closing times vary).
Right by the water's edge, this daytime café serves up a good selection of sandwiches, salads and mains. £
The Green Housekeeper Café
16 Yewdale Road; tel: 015394-41925; daily 9am–6pm.
This popular little café serves breakfast, coffee, lunch and afternoon teas. You'll find excellent home-made scones and cakes, good coffee and light lunches. £
Steam Bistro
Tiberthwaite Avenue; tel: 015394-41928; www.steambistro.co.uk; Tue–Sun dinner only.
Local produce, such as Yew Tree Farm

Galloway beef cooked in red wine, is the key here at this little bistro with a big heart. Set menus with a few daily specials, and bring your own wine policy. £

Hawkshead
Ees Wyke
Near Sawrey; tel: 015394-36393; www.eeswyke.co.uk; daily dinner.
With glorious fell views in the heart of Beatrix Potter country just 2 miles (3km) from Hawkshead, this country house-hotel restaurant serves a daily changing five-course dinner using locally sourced ingredients. £££
The King's Arms
The King's Arms Hotel; tel: 015394-36372; www.kingsarmshawkshead. co.uk; daily noon–2.30pm, 6–9.30pm. Standard but nicely cooked pub food such as steak and burgers served up in a 500-year-old inn. Daily specials provide added interest. ££
The Queen's Head
Main Street; tel: 015394-36271; www.queensheadhawkshead.co.uk; daily noon–2.30pm, 6–9pm.
This old inn serves up imaginative dishes such as slow-cooked Lakeland lamb shoulder, with an emphasis on sourcing very local ingredients. ££

Keswick and Derwent Water.

Tour 4

Keswick to Grasmere

The 31 miles (50km) of this literary tour take you from the key town of Keswick, down the dramatic Thirlmere Valley to the sites associated with William Wordsworth

Keswick, at the top of Derwent Water, is the northern capital of the Lakes. With several small supermarkets, Fair Trade shops and an unsurpassed choice of outdoor clothing outlets, this is a good base for exploring the many lakes and fells, and secluded valleys in the surrounding area.

Just south of Bassenthwaite Lake, Keswick is in range of Skiddaw (locally pronounced *Skidder*), which clears the 3,000ft (900m) contour. Climbing the fell is not difficult, just protracted, and people usually start from Millbeck, near Applethwaite, or from Latrigg. Blencathra, its neighbour, provides a splendid backdrop to the ancient stone circle of Castlerigg.

Highlights

- Museum and Art Gallery
- Cumberland Pencil Museum
- Castlerigg
- Wythburn Church
- St Oswald's Church
- Dove Cottage
- Wordsworth Museum
- Rydal Mount
- St John's in the Vale Church

This route is easily accomplished by public transport, using the regular daily bus service between Keswick and Ambleside. The No. 555 regularly leaves Keswick bus station and the run to Ambleside takes approximately 45 minutes.

Moot Hall in the pedestrianised centre of Keswick.

KESWICK

Keswick ❶ retains a strong Victorian appearance that belies its great age – the name is Old English for 'cheese farm'. About AD 550, St Mungo, first bishop of Glasgow, on hearing that 'many among the mountains were given to idolatry', came and erected a cross as a sign of faith at Crosfeld (Crosthwaite). In the middle of the following century St Herbert became a hermit on one of the islands on nearby Derwent Water, now named after him. It must have been a very remote place then. In 1540 John Leland, the King's antiquarian, arrived to find 'a lytle poore market town cawled Keswike'.

Soon afterwards, however, Keswick became industrialised, when German miners arrived, employed to seek gold but finding only copper. Graphite, discovered in the 16th century and mined in the Seathwaite valley at the head of Borrowdale, has always been useful, but with the invention of the pencil, Keswick assumed world eminence as a centre of pencil production.

Tourism was the next boom. Many visitors were attracted by the Romantic Age towards the end of the 18th century, including Samuel Taylor Coleridge, though as a resident he felt qualified to complain that 'for two thirds of the year we are in...retirement – the other third is alive & swarms with Tourists of all shapes & sizes & characters.'

Halls

Keswick's pedestrianised centre flows around **Moot Hall** or market hall. Built in 1813, it has the grand lines and spired tower of a church (with a one-handed clock). The hall is now the location of Keswick's Tourist and National Park Information Centre (daily 9.30am–5.30pm, closes 4.30pm Nov–Mar).

Market day in Keswick is Saturday, and there is a local produce and craft market specialising in Cumbrian prod-

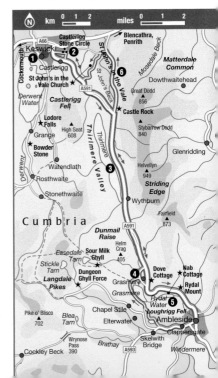

ucts that takes place on most Thursdays of the year.

Five minutes' walk from the town is the Georgian **Greta Hall**, Coleridge's home for three years, until 1803, when the poet Robert Southey moved in and had it for the next 40 years. He thought it the finest single spot in England, as undoubtedly do the present owners, who offer four-star self-catering accommodation (see page 125).

Museums

Keswick's **Museum and Art Gallery** (www.keswickmuseum.org.uk; daily 10am–4pm) has a handy situation in Fitz Park and is a good starting point for anyone with an interest in local traditions. Purpose-built from green volcanic slate, the museum has a delightful Victorian flavour. Following an extensive refurbishment and a new extension, the museum reopened in 2014, with improved accessibility and displays. Among the exhibits are an 1834 scale model of the Lake District, letters by Wordsworth and Southey, and manuscripts from the novelist Hugh Walpole, whose man-

sion, Brackenburn, overlooks Derwent Water.

There are some more unusual museums in the town. One of these is the **Cumberland Pencil Museum** (www.pencilmuseum.co.uk; daily 9.30am–5pm). Celebrating this offshoot of the graphite industry, the museum has surprisingly entertaining displays relating to the mining of graphite and the making of pencils, including the world's largest colouring pencil. There is much here for children to enjoy, including trying out the pencils in the Kids Art Studio.

Another fun exhibition can be found at **Puzzling Place** (www.puzzling place.co.uk; Apr–Oct 11am–5.30pm, school hols opens 10am, Nov–Mar Tue–Sun 11am–5pm, weekends only in Jan), on Museum Square. Full of puzzles and illusions, including holograms, brain teasers and optical illusions, this museum has lots of interactive exhibits. Check out the Anti-Gravity Room, where balls roll up hill and everyone appears to stand at an impossible slant – it's all in the mind!

The puzzles will definitely appeal to children, but it is likely that the tours offered by **Keswick Brewing Company** (www.keswickbrewery.co.uk;

The Keswick Jazz Festival is held every year in May at the Theatre by the Lake.

Taking it all in by the shore of the lake.

tours: Fri, Sat 11am and 2pm; booking advisable) will be of more interest to adults. This microbrewery tour takes visitors around the small plant, explaining the brewing process, and offering samples.

Set on the edge of Derwent Water, the **Theatre by the Lake** (www. theatrebythelake.co.uk) is Keswick's professional theatre company, putting on a series of great productions throughout the year. Sympathetically built of Lakeland stone, the theatre has a 400-seat main hall and a new 100-seat Studio. It also has a café-bar and two gallery spaces catering for temporary exhibitions. One way to reach the theatre is through the attractive Hope Park, which links the town centre with the lake and the theatre.

CASTLERIGG

To the east of Keswick is the stone circle of **Castlerigg** ❷. Here, set on a hill with a wondrous panorama of greater hills all around, well-preserved grey stones form an oval (not a true circle) about 100ft (30m) across. Ten other stones form a rectangle within the circle. The stones

Needle Sports

Keswick has one of the best shops for climbing and outdoor gear in the Lake District, if not the whole country. Needle Sports (daily 9am–5.30pm; www.needlesports.com), on Main Street, has a vast range of equipment, from waterproofs and boots to top-end technical climbing gear. The friendly staff are extremely helpful and are all active climbers, so it is also a good place to head to pick up some local knowledge.

Get all your climbing gear at Needle Sports.

Tranquil Thirlmere, which has a lovely walk all around its shore, is dammed to provide water for the city of Manchester.

are only a 0.5-mile (1km) walk from the outskirts of Keswick.

Castlerigg seems to have had some sort of religious or ceremonial function, as the 38 stones are astronomically aligned. To the Victorian tourists, this was a haunt of Druids, but Castlerigg actually dates back to the much earlier Neolithic age around 3000 BC.

THIRLMERE AND THE FELLS

To venture on beyond Keswick, catch bus No 555 from the bus station. This will take you south, over and around Castlerigg Fell and down into the valley of Thirlmere.

Just after crossing St John's Beck, several high points come into view. On the left is craggy **Castle Rock** guarding the entrance to St John's in the Vale. The Helvellyn range rises to the east, with Great Dodd crowning the skyline at 2,807ft (856m), and the mighty **Helvellyn** itself (3,116ft/950m; see page 31). The King's Head hotel at **Thirlspot Inn** on the left is one of several starting points from which an ascent of Helvellyn might begin.

Thirlmere ❸, 4 miles (6.5km) long, may be circumnavigated by the

quiet road around its shores, and it makes a pleasant and unstrenuous bike ride. A plaque on the dam commemorates the beginning of work on the reservoir (22 August 1890), which grew from two small lakes, Leathe's Water and Wythburn Water. The

Castlerigg stone circle, 100ft (30m) in diameter, contains 38 stones, the tallest 7.5ft (2.3m) high.

Hey-ho for the open road at Dunmail Raise.

dam holds the water to a depth of 50ft (15m); which is much deeper than the original lakes had been. Thirlmere feeds the water taps of Manchester, some 98 miles (158km) to the south.

At times of low water, the bare shoreline may appear rather unsightly, but the plantations that once stood like battalions of soldiers at attention are a lot more varied now. Red deer inhabit the woodlands west of the water, and they spend the summer on the open fells beyond.

Wythburn Church (pronounced Wyburn, meaning a valley where willow trees grow) is visible on the eastern shore of the lake. The building, which is long, low and predominantly 17th-century, has retained its charming old Lake District flavour.

Ancient pass

The road continues south, crossing the watershed at **Dunmail Raise**. This ancient pass between Thirlmere and Grasmere is now a stretch of dual carriageway. A cairn at the top, between the carriageways, explains the name of the pass. It marks where Dunmail, the last king of Cumberland,

was defeated in AD 945 by Edmund, King of Northumbria, and was, until 1974, on the border of Cumberland and Westmorland.

There is a good view on the right of the rugged 'mane' of Helm Crag from the lay-by on Dunmail Raise. Reaching the summit demands rock-climbing skills and nerve. Wainwright, in his famous pictorial guide to the area, left a space on which he might write the date of his ascent, but he never managed that last awkward bit.

In the days of the first tourists, coachmen driving four-in-hands from Windermere to Keswick entertained their passengers by giving names to unusual rocks, which have remained, such as the **Lion and the Lamb**, at the southern end of the ridge.

Woodland Trails

Nature trails are to be found in the woodland on either side of Thirlmere at Swirls, Launchy Gill and Harrop. Wildlife you might see includes red deer and red squirrels. The woodland is being diversified from the conifers planted earlier to include native species.

Red squirrels can still be found in the wild in the Lake District.

The Raise allows people to hear as well as see further. In the early 19th century, during the Peninsular War when news was eagerly await-ed, Thomas De Quincey and William Wordsworth walked up the Raise from Grasmere one night, to meet the Keswick carrier bringing the Lon-don papers. Wordsworth lay on the ground and listened to 'catch any sound of wheels that might be groan-ing along at a distance'.

GRASMERE

Grasmere ❹, the name of both town and lake, is the heart of 'Wordsworthshire', and it can be very busy during high season. The over-flowing car parks near Stock Lane are by the field in which the **Grasmere Sports** have been held in August for more than 130 years. There were traffic problems when Beatrix Potter visited the Sports in 1895, for she was

a late arrival 'and had difficulty in find-ing friends among the crowd of car-riages'. As instigator of the Lonsdale Belt prize for British boxers, the Fifth Earl of Lonsdale took special interest in the Cumberland and Westmorland style of wrestling, arriving from his Lowther estate via Kirkstone Pass in a yellow-painted coach.

Grasmere (the lake, that is, com-plete with island and rowing boats) lies in a kind of a mountain urn as the Vale of Grasmere is ringed almost completely by shapely fells, of which the most prominent is Helm Crag. In the hamlet of Grasmere on the north side of the lake is a pleasant stop with a number of little shops.

St Oswald's Church remains much as it was in Wordsworth's time, a structure of 'rude and antique maj-esty, pillars crowded and the roof upheld, By naked rafters intricately crossed'. The annual Rushbearing, on a Saturday in mid or late July (see page 65), was a feature of the poet's day, when he recorded seeing children, each with a garland, walking through the still churchyard. Wordsworth and many of his family members are bur-ied here.

St Oswald's rustic church. Wordsworth's Bible is in a glass case by the altar.

The fire makes the Wordsworths' Dove Cottage, once the village inn, look snug. In reality, the rooms were small and cramped for the growing family.

Dove Cottage

The home of William Wordsworth during his early, highly creative years, from 1799–1808, **Dove Cottage** (www.wordsworth.org.uk; tours daily 9.30am–5pm, 4pm in winter, also closed Tue in Feb and Dec) stands just to the east of the main road, in an area known as Town End. Now hemmed in by buildings, the whitewashed cottage then had a view directly over Grasmere, and William would lie at night with the curtains open, so he could see the moon on the water.

The cottage rooms are rather cramped, and it is hard to imagine how William, his sister Dorothy, wife Mary (a childhood friend he married in 1802) and friends fitted in. But it is particularly appealing in cold weather, when a bright fire burns in the grate.

The **Wordsworth Museum** (same times and ticket as the cottage), in an adjacent barn conversion, hous-

Grasmere Gingerbread

The Grasmere Gingerbread shop (www.grasmeregingerbread.co.uk; Mon–Sat 9.15am–5pm, Sun 12.30–4.30pm, opens daily 12.30pm winter and school terms) has been selling its famous product since the 1850s, when local cook Sarah Nelson began making the cakes for tourists. The biscuit-like gingerbread is still made to the original recipe, and the tiny shop retains its 19th-century charm. The shop also sells award-winning rum butter.

Gingerbread makes a good Grasmere souvenir.

The beautifully landscaped Edwardian gardens at Rydal Hall offer wonderful views over the Rothay Valley.

es a permanent exhibition recounting the Wordsworth story and is backed up by special exhibitions.

RYDAL WATER

Grasmere and Rydal Water are connected by a level footpath called **Loughrigg Terrace**. The path can be reached directly from Dove Cottage along a causeway by the road that offers unhindered views of the lake and Helm Crag or via a wood called

Camping at Loughrigg Tarn, one of the small lakes near Grasmere.

Bainbriggs, a favourite pre-tea walk of the Wordsworths. Alternatively, start from near the church, and walk around the other side of the lake. After a little road work, a footpath is found that leads to the south of the two lakes.

Rydal Water ❺, which is smaller than Grasmere, is a reedy lake, with several islands and a population of waterfowl. Red squirrels might be seen in the larches. The view for much of the year is given a ginger hue by the dead bracken fronds.

Rydal Mount

At the head of the village, near the start of a footpath leading back to Grasmere, is **Rydal Mount** (www.rydalmount.co.uk; Mar–Oct daily 9.30am–5pm, Nov–Dec, Feb Wed–Sun 11am–4pm). William and Mary Wordsworth lived here from 1813 until their deaths in 1850 and 1855, caring for William's sister, Dorothy, for her last 20 years. In the house you can see the living room and bedrooms, all with original items of furniture, as well as portraits of the Wordsworths. The gardens remain much as they were when laid out by Wordsworth

William Wordsworth

The poet William Wordsworth (1770–1850) was one of the instigators and leading lights of British Romanticism. He was born in Cockermouth and, after travels in Europe where he witnessed the French Revolution, spent the last 50 years of his life in Grasmere and Rydal, becoming Poet Laureate in 1843. He was loyally supported by his sister Dorothy (1771–1855), and her *Grasmere Journal* sheds light on both her and their life and work.

Dove Cottage, the Wordsworths' home before Rydal Mount.

and have great views over the nearby lakes. A descendant now owns the property, and visitors can book special evening guided tours of the house and 4.5-acre (2-hectare) garden, which was landscaped by Wordsworth.

St Mary's Church, built in 1824, contains a memorial to Dr Thomas Arnold, his wife and son Matthew, as well as a plaque dedicated to Wordsworth, who worshipped here. The church is adjacent to **Dora's Field**, which Wordsworth bought and gave to

Postbox in a dry-stone wall, handy for postcards home.

his daughter, Dora. When she died aged 39 (three of William and Mary's five children predeceased them), Wordsworth planted daffodils here. In April there's an expanse of daffodils and narcissi – if the sheep haven't got to them first.

Rydal Hall, home of the Le Flemings in Wordsworth's day, is now a conference and study centre for Carlisle Diocese. The Edwardian gardens with Italianate terracing are of considerable importance and are being restored. They and the tea shop (www.rydalhall.org; daily 10am–5pm, closes earlier in winter) are open to the public, and a footpath to Ambleside passes through the park.

Nab Cottage

Across Rydal Water is Nab Cottage (www.nabcottage.com), once secluded but now a language school. Thomas De Quincey lodged here and then married Peggy Simpson, the daughter of his landlord. Wordsworth thought that De Quincey could have done better, but the happy couple remained content and moved to Wordsworth's old cottage at Grasmere, while Nab Cottage became home to Hartley Coleridge, the son of Samuel Taylor Coleridge.

Hikers hit the heights of Blencathra, whose shape has given it the name Saddleback. There are magnificent views in all directions.

BACK TO KESWICK

If you have your own transport you can carry on to Ambleside (see page 35) and double back in a loop that will provide you with glorious views over the fells. Head through Clappersgate and turn right before Skelwith Bridge up a signposted road that crosses **Red Bank** (which has a fine view of Grasmere lake) and back to Grasmere town. From here the road heads back along Thirlmere the same way you came.

You can pick up the bus back to Keswick in either Grasmere or Ambleside. At the northern end of Thirlmere a right turn heads down to a valley called **St John's in the Vale** ⑥. The crag on the right is known as **Castle Rock**, and it greatly impressed early tourists. William Hutchinson (1774) compared it with 'an ancient ruined castle' and Walter Scott, shown the rock and having read Hutchinson's account, wrote *The Bridal of Triermain*, a poem in which King Arthur finds the castle deserted, rouses it with a bugle blast and brings it to life, with 'a band of damsels fair'.

If you have time at the end of the tour it is well worth exploring the vale, on foot or by bike. When the high fells are powdered with snow it is an almost alpine spectacle, for the eye goes directly to **Blencathra** (2,847ft/868m), which appears to block out half the sky. John Ruskin, who climbed Blencathra in 1867, thought of it as 'the finest thing I've yet seen, there being several bits of real crag-work and a fine view at the top over the great plain of Penrith on one side, and the Cumberland hills, as

St John's in the Vale Church, made over by the Victorians with an altar by Sir Gilbert Scott.

a chain, on the other. Fine fresh wind blowing, and plenty of crows.'

St John's in the Vale Church

Two miles (3km) down this valley, look for the sign to **St John's in the Vale Church**. A narrow road leads to the church, which sits snugly behind yew trees in the shadow of a steep hill. A church on the site was mentioned in a document dated 1554, but the present structure dates from 1845. One of the finely lettered

Farm nestled amongst the hills.

tombstones in the churchyard is dedicated to John Richardson (1817–86), whose poems in the Lakeland dialect are still very much enjoyed.

Eating Out

Keswick

The George Hotel
St John's Street; tel: 017687-72076; www.georgehotelkeswick.co.uk; daily dinner only.
The town's oldest inn has a decent restaurant serving hearty food in large portions, including the famous George Cow Pie. ££

Highfield Restaurant
Highfield Hotel, The Heads; tel: 017687-72508; www.highfield keswick.co.uk; daily 6.30–8.30pm (reservations essential).
This award-winning restaurant is one of the best in the area. Very good modern British food – think pan-fried scallops with baby black pudding and smoked pancetta or seared collop of Cumberland beef – using local ingredients. ££

The Old Keswickian
Market Square; tel: 017687-73861; www.oldkeswickian.co.uk; Mon–Thu 11am–10.30pm, Fri–Sat 11am–11.40pm, Sun 11am–11pm (earlier closure in winter).
The best fish and chip shop in town, with a sit-down restaurant upstairs (daily 11am–8.30pm, earlier closure Sun and winter). Very tasty, fresh and local fish, as well as great

home-made meat pies using prime Lakeland beef. £

Sienna's
21 Station Street; tel: 017687-80430; www.siennasbarandgrill.com; bar daily noon–11pm (midnight Tue–Sat), restaurant daily 5.30–9.30pm.
The upstairs steak house at Sienna's has great local meat. ££

Stalls Bar
Theatre by the Lake, Lakeside; tel: 017687-81102; daily 10am–9pm (11pm on performance nights).
A great bet for coffee and cakes, light lunches, afternoon teas, pre-theatre meals or post-performance drinks. £

Grasmere and Rydal

The Jumble Room
Langdale Road; tel: 015394-35188; www.thejumbleroom.co.uk; Wed–Mon 5.30pm–9.30pm.
A highly recommended eatery, serving up great food from crab crostini to Peking chicken. ££

The Old School Room Tea Shop
Rydal Hall; tel: 015394-32050; www.rydalhall.org/tea-shop; daily 10am–5pm (closes earlier in winter).
The lovely home-made cakes and sandwiches here make it a good choice for lunch or afternoon tea. £

Festivals

Lakeland has its distinct set of outdoor celebrations, from Shepherds' Meets and traditional sports to events that make the most of the Lakes themselves

For centuries, the Lake District proper was a secluded, little-known corner of England, too close to the Scottish border for comfort, and keeping largely to itself. Because of this, it developed a lively local culture and identity, still evident in its many fairs and festivals.

LOCAL LORE

Sheep farming formed the focus of many festivals, and Shepherds' Meets, when traditionally stray sheep from the 'gathering' were returned to their rightful owners, are still held today. These can include hound-trailing, where the dogs follow a scent laid down by a man dragging a sack, and much eating of tatie pot, a meat and potato stew. Today the Lakes's biggest country event is the two-day Game & Country Fair held every August at Lowther.

Cumberland and Westmorland wrestling demands brains as well as brawn and began with school lads 'takking 'od' (taking hold) on a village green. Such wrestling became respectable when it was to be seen at the Grasmere Sports, held in August, and patronised by the Earls of Lonsdale from Lowther Park.

Kendal's Mintfest is one of the UK's leading international street arts festivals.

Diary of Events

The following is just a selection of the many events that take place during the year (see the Fairs and Festivals section of www.golakes.co.uk for more listings).

Rushbearing: These traditional processions to church, accompanied by hymn singing, take place in Ambleside and Grasmere in July.

Derwentwater Regatta: In July boats of all kinds take to the water for aquatic-themed events and water mayhem in King Pocky's Regatta (www.nationaltrust.org.uk/borrowdale).

The Cumberland Show: This takes place in June every year, with livestock displays, local produce and Lakeland games (www.cumberland show.co.uk).

Grasmere Lakeland Sports and Show: If you want to see traditional wrestling and fell races, this is the event to head for, held in late August (www.grasmeresports.com).

The World's Biggest Liar Competition: In November, fibbers big and small descend on the Bridge Inn, Santon Bridge, to persuade others of their tall tales (www.santonbridgeinn.com).

More bizarre events include 'gurning through a braffin' – pulling the funniest face through a horse-collar, which survives at Egremont – and an idiosyncratic competition to find t'biggest liar at Santon Bridge keeps alive a tradition dating back to Will Ritson, of Wasdale Head, a teller of outrageous tales.

The Church has conserved much of the local culture. The Rushbearing dates back to the days when churches had earthen floors and on a specified day freshly cut rushes were spread on the ground. Rushbearings at Ambleside and Grasmere attract large crowds.

SUMMER FUN

Less traditional are the summer festivals put on for holidaymakers, such as the Lake District Summer Music Festival, with performances of first-class classical music, and Derwentwater Regatta for fun in boats held in July.

Looking south into Borrowdale.

Tour 5

Borrowdale and Buttermere

Borrowdale is one of the most attractive valleys in all of Lakeland, and this 20-mile (32km) tour from Keswick passes through the dale and over the Honister Pass

Borrowdale is a star of the northern Lakes. Centred on the village of Grange, the valley comes skittering down from England's highest mountain, 3,209ft (978m) Scafell Pike, leading the lovely, bubbling River Derwent into the majestic Derwent Water at Keswick. It offers demanding crags for rock-climbing and airy ridges with views for walkers.

It has long been a favourite tourist destination. Canon Rawnsley, the Keswick parson and a founder of the National Trust, considered there was 'no better five shillings' worth of carriage driving at the Lakes than can be enjoyed by all who gather in the Keswick Market Place on a fine morning at ten o'clock and take their seats on any of the char-a-bancs waiting to

Highlights

- Derwent Water
- Lodore Falls
- Bowder Stone
- Sour Milk Ghyll
- Honister Pass
- Honister Slate Mine
- Great Gable
- Buttermere
- Newlands

convey them up Borrowdale, thence home by the Newlands Vale.'

Able-bodied passengers were asked to walk up steep hills. On descents, a squeal emanated from the 'slipper' or wedge of wood under the wheel used as a braking device.

Enjoying a walk around the shores of Derwent Water.

calm it mirrors a range of handsome fells and the Jaws of Borrowdale, best seen from Friar's Crag (on the right as you leave Keswick).

The walks around the shores of the lake are well laid out and offer incredible views.

Part of the attraction of the lake is its few islands. The largest is **Derwent Island**, owned by the National Trust. Once the property of Furness Abbey, after the dissolution it was sold by the Crown to the Company of Mines Royal, and in the 16th century German miners, whose skills were needed to recover local copper, lived here. In the 18th century, the lovely Italianate Derwent Island House was here – much to Wordsworth's disgust – and it opens open to the general public five days a year.

Lake cruises

As well as rowing boats, self-drive motorboats and other pleasure craft, there is a regular service to various jetties, and one of the most pleasant ways to explore the lake is by taking one of the scheduled services run by the **Keswick Launch Company** (www.

Coach-drivers gave a running commentary on what was to be seen and made up tales about the locals, such as how they constructed a wall across the bottom of the valley to restrain the cuckoo and ensure everlasting summer.

For those without a car, Borrowdale is easily accessed by public transport from Keswick. Buses Nos. 78 (the 'Borrowdale Bus') and 77 and 77A ('Honister Rambler') all run regular services past Derwent Water and on into the valley, the latter going on across the fierce Honister Pass.

DERWENT WATER

From Keswick bus station take the No. 78 (daily, limited winter service), which follows the romantic road running through Borrowdale. The road leaves Keswick to skirt **Derwent Water ❶** on its eastern bank. Known as the 'queen' of English lakes, the 3-mile (5km) long body of water looks shallow but actually has a maximum depth of 72ft (22m). When it is

Picture-perfect – spectacular reflections on Derwent Water, with Friar's Crag in the background.

keswick-launch.co.uk). Two services run daily, clockwise and anticlockwise, around the lake, leaving every hour on the hour (first sailings 10am and 9.45am respectively; fewer sailings in winter). One option is to take the boat from Keswick to Lodore and pick up the bus to carry on down Borrowdale from there.

LODORE FALLS

Near the head of Derwent Water, located behind the Lodore Falls Hotel and accessible on payment of a small charge, you'll find the **Lodore Falls**, about which Robert Southey wrote *The Cataract of Lodore* (1820): 'Collecting, projecting, Receding and speeding, And shocking and rocking/ And darting and parting…'

A visit to the falls is exciting in wet spells but they are less impressive during periods of dry weather. It is said that an American, after looking for them for several hours, sat down and asked a passer-by, 'Say, where are the Lodore Falls?' They informed him that he was sitting on them.

GRANGE-IN-BORROWDALE

A narrow, double bridge leads to **Grange-in-Borrowdale ❷** (grange, as this is where the granary of Furness Abbey was located). The **church** here, built in 1871 with imitation Norman dogtooth decoration, is picturesque. About a mile from Grange on

The Keswick Launch Company runs year-round and offers 50-minute trips around Derwent Water.

Pausing to take in the splendour of his surroundings.

Borrowdale has long been one of the top rock-climbing destinations in the Lakes. The proximity of the crags to the valley floor means they are easy to reach and perfect for a spot of late-afternoon summer climbing when the rock has been warmed by the sun. There are some classic routes here, including the wonderful *Little Chamonix* on Shepherds Crag, as well as some state-of-the-art test pieces for the professional climbers.

the road running west of Derwent Water is **Brackenburn**, a private house once owned by Hugh Walpole, author of *The Herries Chronicle*, three books published in the 1930s, about a Cumberland boy. Above the garage, where he had a study with 30,000 books, is a blue plaque. To him, this was a 'little paradise on Cat Bells', the fell looming beyond. Water drawn from deep in the fell is said to have the effect of good wine.

Grange is a good point from which to walk beside the **River Derwent**, its pure water tinged green by pieces of greenish slate on the river bed, and through the famous Borrowdale sessile oak woods.

Boulders and scree

Continue on down the valley to where a sign heralds the **Bowder Stone**, an enormous boulder with a length of 62ft (19m) and a height of 36ft (11m). Although a wooden ladder with rails, fixed against the side of the stone, gives access to its summit, you will often see rock climbers tack-

ling the difficult bouldering problems on the rock. The ones that come out from under the overhang are particularly strenuous.

The road continues, pent-in between **King's How** (named after Edward VII) and **Castle Crag**, which looms above the oak woods on the west bank and is best approached from Grange. Climbing its steep scree slope is not to be undertaken lightly, but with care visitors can reach a supreme vantage point with magnificent

If you take your dog on a walk, make sure to keep it on a lead if there are farm animals around.

Eagle Crag near Stonethwaite. A dry-stone wall helps walkers find their way between here and neighbouring Sergeant's Crag.

views overlooking the oak-wooded valley, Derwent Water and Skiddaw.

The village of **Rosthwaite** ❸, with a post office and a popular village store, is at the start of a footpath leading over the adjacent fell to the remote hamlet of **Watendlath**, which lies beside a tarn and is owned by the National Trust.

Beyond Rosthwaite is **Stonethwaite**, a hamlet worth exploring. Both communities were named by Norse settlers for the amount of stone lying about, all of which had to be cleared before cultivation.

The way up Honister Pass is steep but passes through some of the area's most spectacular scenery.

EAGLE CRAG

Walking up the dale for a short distance brings 1,706ft (520m) **Eagle Crag** into view. The golden eagles of Eagle Crag died out, as elsewhere in England, in the mid-19th century. Their eggs were stolen, and a bounty paid on dead birds can be found in parish records. A pair returned to breed in the Lake District in 1969, but the female has not been seen since 2004. However, the same male was seen displaying to attract a mate in 2014.

GRAPHITE MINES

The dale peters out at **Seathwaite Farm**, a mile south of Seatoller, left down a side road. The wettest inhabited farm in England (125ins/3,175mm a year), Seathwaite has been tended by four generations of Edmondsons and has a campsite.

A short walk from Seathwaite Farm is **Stockley Bridge**, a packhorse-type bridge on the route from Borrowdale to Wasdale. There is also a track from Seathwaite barn across the valley to a river bridge, from which an approach may be made to the waterfalls of **Sour Milk Ghyll** ❹. On the hillside are remains of the old graphite mines,

HONISTER PASS

Able-bodied men taking the Borrowdale Coach Round in the 19th century had to walk up **Honister Pass** ❻ (1,190ft/363m) from Seatoller. Canon Rawnsley, arriving at the head of the pass, saw **Honister Crag**, which 'gleams at us as if some great earth painter had been grinding up grey slate and mixed it with emerald and begun to wash in his colour from skyline to the valley bottom.' The slate quarried up here was composed of the compacted dust and ash from volcanic activity.

A rough track now runs up the side of Honister Crag, and there is

which are too hazardous to explore. When a pure form of graphite was discovered here in the 16th century, it had various uses. A rare mineral, it was used to make metal castings and cannon balls, and it was treated like gold. In the early 19th century, guards were posted at the mines, and workmen were searched before they left. The graphite eventually created Keswick's pencil industry.

SEATOLLER

From Rosthwaite there is ready access to the banks of the River Derwent. Of special interest, west of the river and between Rosthwaite and Seatoller, is the lovely oak woodland, **Johnny Wood**, in which there is a nature trail.

From the riverside you can walk up the dale to **Seatoller** ❺, a cluster of attractive buildings, some erected for quarrymen, when the Honister mines were first opened. The National Park authority has converted a barn into a shop and information point.

If you are using public transport from Seatoller, you must change bus from the No. 78 to continue on to Buttermere. The 77A runs daily (Easter–Oct) from Seatoller to Keswick via Lorton and Whinlatter, with the 77 doing the reverse route.

Borrowdale Woodland

The woodlands of Borrowdale, a 'Special Area of Conservation', are the biggest area of sessile oak (Quercus petraea) in northern England. The oaks are the largest of the native broadleaf trees and support a host of wildlife, from dormice to butterflies. In Borrowdale there are also small tracts of rare 'bog woodland', with birch, alder and ash. These areas are rich in wild flowers.

The oaks provide a habitat for a huge variety of wildlife.

little to indicate that the whole fell is honeycombed by shafts and galleries. For a time, it was customary to pack slate on long sledges and run with the sledges down the screes to the road-side below. The sledgeman then had to climb back with his sledge for an-other load.

Honister Slate Mine

One of the mines is still operational and welcomes visitors. At **Honis-ter Slate Mine** (www.honister. com; daily 9am–5pm) you can pick up a helmet and lamp and venture underground on guided tours (dai-ly 10.30am, 12.30pm and 3.30pm; also 2pm and book in advance in high season) to see the workings and huge caverns from which the slate has been extracted. If you are feel-ing particularly adventurous, then try out the mine's via *ferrata* ('iron way', a series of metal ladders fixed to the rock protected by steel cables; extra charge). This is only for those with a

Visitors to Honister Slate Mine, where Westmorland Green has been extracted for centuries.

head for heights, as it winds up the crag face, high above the pass, to the top of Fleetwith Pike (2,126ft/ 648m). A whole community lived in cave-like rooms etched out of

Great Gable lies at the heart of the northern Lakes. It can be reached from many directions and it offers some of the finest views in the area.

The Fish Inn, formerly Fish Hotel, where Mary Robinson found fame as The Maid of Buttermere.

the rock at the top. The Via Ferrata Xtreme is the ultimate challenge.

The mine has a café and shop.

Great Gable

Fell walkers can head off from the summit of the Honister Pass to follow a comparatively easy route to the summit of **Great Gable** (2,949ft/899m). On Remembrance Sunday, many gather beside a memorial on Great Gable to remember those members of the Fell and Rock Climbing Club who died in the two world wars.

BUTTERMERE

The road descends from the heights of Honister to **Buttermere** ❼, which is reached at Gatesgarth Farm at the foot of shapely **Fleetwith Pike** (2,126ft/648m). Stop beside the farm if you wish to explore the dalehead. Others go on to the **The Fish Inn** at Buttermere village, which once had a reputation for strong ale. The lake is small, only 1.5 miles (2.5km) long and 0.75 mile (1km wide), but is exceptionally attractive, surrounded by high fells.

The Buttermere Beauty

The tale of Mary Robinson is told in Melvyn Bragg's *The Maid of Buttermere*. She was the daughter of a landlord of The Fish Inn and was noted for her looks. This 'Buttermere Beauty' was 15, when Joseph Budworth, an early travel guide writer, first saw her on 1792 and made her famous. Mary attracted the attention of a 'gentleman' who introduced himself as the Hon. Alexander Hope MP, brother of the Earl of Hopetoun. They were married in 1802. Unfortunately, the Hon. Alexander turned out to be

Buttermere Church

The present St James's Church in Buttermere dates from 1840. On a window ledge is a plaque in memory of Alfred Wainwright, the most famous of fell walkers and author of the idiosyncratic Pictorial Guides to the Lake District fells. Look through the window on a clear day and the fell named Hay Stacks is in view. After Wainwright's death in 1991, his ashes were scattered on Hay Stacks at his particular request.

The church, above Buttermere, remembers Alfred Wainwright.

Buttermere, looking across to Fleetwith Pike. The 2- to 3-hour walk around the lake, with wonderful views of the fells, makes this a popular destination.

John Hatfield, an imposter, bigamist, forger and bankrupt. His iniquities led to him being hanged at Carlisle. The Buttermere Beauty later married a local farmer.

Around the lake

The walk around Buttermere lake takes 2–3 hours and is one of the finest valley walks in Lakeland, with spectacular views of the surrounding

River in the Newlands valley after heavy rainfall.

fells as well as the still waters of the lake. Although the footpath is fairly obvious all the way round, a board at Buttermere shows the route, which at one point passes through a Victorian tunnel cut into the rock. For the best views the walk is best done clockwise.

There are other good walks from here, including one to **Hay Stacks** (1,958ft/597m), which was one of Alfred Wainwright's favourite fells.

NEWLANDS

To explore a little further from the lake, follow the road up the steep hill past Buttermere's church of St James for about a mile (1.5km). This will bring you to **Newlands Hause** ❽, the high point of the road at 1,093ft (333m). This used to be a struggle for the coach horses, and passengers would be asked to walk beside the coach in order to lighten the load. Close by, to the south of the road, are the waterfalls of Moss Force.

Old headstones lined up in Littletown Church graveyard, in the Newlands Valley.

Newlands is a secluded valley, almost a basin among fells, with many farms and two tiny hamlets, Stair and Little Town, which was well known to Beatrix Potter, who included drawings of it in *The Tale of Mrs Tiggy-Winkle*.

The mine shafts driven into the flanks of **Cat Bells** and **Maiden Moor** were worked as far back as the days of Queen Elizabeth I. They yielded copper, lead and even a little gold. Cat Bells is one of the Lakes' most popular mountain fell walks, as it has fantastic views over Derwent Water and Newlands, and back towards Keswick, Skiddaw and Saddleback.

If you have your own transport, you can carry on through the pretty Newlands valley down to Derwent Water and then to Keswick. If you are relying on public transport, however, return to Buttermere, where you can pick up either bus No. 77 or 77A back to Keswick.

Eating Out

Borrowdale
Borrowdale Gates
Grange-in-Borrowdale; tel: 017687-77204; www.borrowdale-gates.com; daily 6.30–8.30pm, Sun noon–1.45pm.
An excellent place for dinner or Sunday lunch, the Gates uses local ingredients to great effect in its French-inspired cooking. £££
The Langstrath
Stonethwaite; tel: 017687-77239; www.thelangstrath.com; daily lunch and dinner.
This very pleasant inn has good local beers and a menu that concentrates on well-cooked Lakeland dishes. ££
The Scafell Hotel
Rosthwaite; tel: 017687-77208; www.scafell.co.uk; daily lunch.
The lunchtime bar menu at the Scafell offers tasty and good-value meals, as well as an appealing children's menu. £

Buttermere
The Bridge Hotel and Inn
The Bridge Hotel; tel: 017687-70252; www.bridge-hotel.com; daily noon–9.30pm.
The pub serves dishes including Cumberland sausages, Lakeland hot pot and steak and ale pie. The more sophisticated hotel dining room offers such delights as locally caught trout. ££
The Fish Inn
The Fish Inn; tel: 017687-70253; www.fishinnbuttermere.co.uk; daily noon–2pm, 6–9pm (check in winter).
The bar meals are hearty and tasty, with the usual selection of Cumberland sausages and lamb dishes. ££

Newlands
Swinside Lodge
Swinside Lodge Hotel; tel: 017687-72948; www.swinsidelodge-hotel.co.uk; dinner daily.
Book in advance for the daily-changing four-course set dinner. £££

Fell ponies, once used for light farm work, near Caldbeck.

Tour 6

Around Skiddaw

This 60-mile (97km) round trip from Keswick takes you into the less well-known country beyond the great fell of Skiddaw, with an optional side trip to towns on the coast

Skiddaw slate gives this northern fell country grand, sweeping lines. Its lofty height is Old Skiddaw, topping the 3,000ft (900m) contour and sprawling over an area of 14 sq miles (36 sq km). 'Back o' Skidder' is a good, if austere, path from near the old Sanatorium at Threlkeld to Skiddaw House, among great flocks of sheep. Skiddaw House, built for the use of shepherds, is now a youth hostel in season (www.skiddawhouse.co.uk; Mar–Oct 5pm–10am). Pre-booked guests can use the 'Refuge' to shelter outside opening hours.

Follow the sweep of hills from Mosedale beside the River Caldew to the cul-de-sac of what remains of mining days at the highly mineralised hill called Carrock Fell to enjoy great views far south into the valley where Thirlmere lies.

Highlights

- Blencathra
- Threlkeld
- Caldbeck
- Wordsworth House and Garden
- Jennings Brewery
- Maryport
- Whitehaven
- Bassenthwaite Lake
- Mirehouse

In the churchyard of Caldbeck lie the mortal remains of huntsman John Peel (see page 79), who in the song had a coat so grey – the undyed wool of the Herdwick sheep. Westwards lies the market town of Cockermouth and classic Lake District terrain, with

Stick to the marked paths.

soaring fells reflected in Loweswater and Crummock Water.

This route can be done by public transport. There is a bus service that circles Skiddaw, and connections to the coast.

BLENCATHRA

If catching a bus, take the Calbeck Rambler 73A (some daily services Easter–Oct but check for times) from Keswick bus station. The view to the north of the road is dominated by **Blencathra** (2,847ft/868m, see page 62), a majestic fell that turns purple with flowering heather in late summer. Walkers who begin in Threlkeld and start with a walk through the fields at the foot of the great hill usually pick the path on the ridge that leads directly to the summit. In a strong wind, avoid this route. Coleridge, one of the Lakeland Poets, appreciated the power of moving air: 'On stern Blencathra's perilous height, The winds are tyrannous and strong; And flashing forth unsteady light, From stern Blencathra's skiey height, As loud the torrents throng!'

THRELKELD

Tucked under the slopes of Blencathra is the small village of **Threlkeld ❶**. Visit the **Quarry and Mining Museum** (www.threlkeldquarryand miningmuseum.co.uk; Easter–Oct daily 10am–5pm) just 1 mile (1.5km) along the road to St John's in the Vale. There are old mine shafts and an exhibition explaining how the valuable minerals were extracted, plus a chance to tour a mine and an artificial caving system to explore. There is a large outdoor display of mining machinery, and the steam railway takes visitors between quarries.

MUNGRISDALE

Back on the A66, a little way after Threlkeld, turn left along the valley of the River Glenderamackin. This brings you to **Mungrisdale ❷**. The **church** here, dedicated to St Kentigern (St

St Kentigern in Mungrisdale Church is a simple church with a complicated three-decker pulpit.

Climbing Skiddaw

The 10-mile (16km) round trip up Skiddaw (3,054ft/931m) from Keswick is straightforward, marked by good paths all the way. To the north of the town, take the footpath behind Latrigg Fell and then turn left up the valley of Whit Beck. This path will take you all the way to the summit. Although it is a relatively easy walk, make sure you have good boots and clothing, as in bad weather conditions it can be very grim up here indeed.

The paths up Skiddaw are gentle enough, but it's still a long walk.

Mungo), is an architectural treasure dating from the 18th century. Long and low, with a whitewashed interior, it has a three-decker pulpit dated 1679. The clerk sat on the lower deck, while the parson took the service from the second deck and then stepped up to preach from the top deck.

Carry on to **Mosedale** into an area that has the grand, open feel of the countryside Back o' Skiddaw. The scenic valley has the atmosphere of a Scottish glen: boulders, heather and a tumbling beck – crossed at one point by a private bridge that gives access to a walk to **Bowscale Tarn** – in a grand setting of fells.

Where the road peters out, there are the remains of a mine at **Carrock Fell** (2,174ft/663m). In 1857, Carrock was visited by Charles Dickens and Wilkie Collins, though local people had told them no visitors ever went up that hill. The two men had arrived on a wet day, and at the top, in mist and rain, there was no view to be seen.

CALDBECK

On to **Caldbeck** ❸ (meaning cold stream), which drew much of its past prosperity from industries powered by the fast-flowing River Caldew. The village was once full of working mills, one of which has been restored and has a café. The area is a vast sheep range also inhabited by some of the stocky, dark fell-type ponies once ridden by the shepherds and used for light farm work. Caldbeck, built largely of limestone, is on the northern boundary of the Lake District National Park. Ask locally for directions to the **Howk**, a limestone gorge popularly thought of as a place for fairy revels, hence the alternative name Fairykirk.

Famous huntsman

John Peel, the huntsman of the song, was born at Park End in 1776 and interred in the Caldbeck churchyard in 1854. Hunting symbols are found on his large gravestone not far from the church door. The words that have gone round the world in the song *D'ye Ken John Peel* were composed by John Woodcock Graves, a great friend of Peel and a fellow huntsman. Peel's portrait is kept in the local pub, the Oddfellows' Arms, as is the only known portrait of Graves.

Caldbeck grew rich on its many industrial mills, driven by the fast-flowing River Caldew.

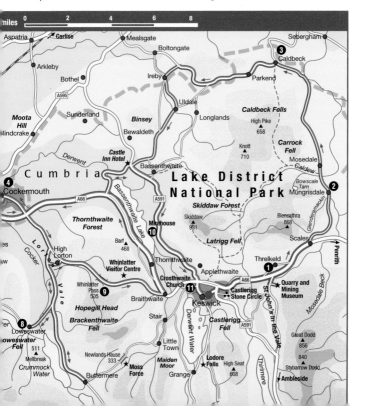

Cockermouth is where Wordsworth was born, and a large part of the 18th- and 19th-century centre of the town remains as it was then.

John Peel was first sung in 1824 in Gate House in Caldbeck, Graves's home, to the tune of a Border rant called *Bonnie Annie*. A different version of the music was composed in 1869 by William Metcalfe, the choirmaster of Carlisle Cathedral. Metcalfe's tune survived to be the one we enjoy today.

COCKERMOUTH

The road continues over the back of the fell country to the 4-star Castle Inn

Jennings Brewery lies between Cockermouth Castle and where the rivers Cocker and Derwent merge.

Hotel. Join the A66 towards Cockermouth. The Caldbeck Rambler bus carries on by the side of Bassenthwaite Lake and back to Keswick. To head for Cockermouth, change at Castle Inn to bus X4/X5 (limited service from this stop, check beforehand for times).

At the confluence of the Cocker and Derwent rivers is the market town of **Cockermouth ❹**. It stands back from Lakeland proper, and its red sandstone buildings emphasise its peripheral status. It was given a market charter in 1221, but there is no regular market here today. Cockermouth suffered devastating flooding and damage to its historic buildings and bridges in 2009, when the rivers Derwent and Cocker overflowed following heavy rainfall, but following a model reconstruction, most of the damage has now been repaired.

The broad, tree-lined main street is relatively quiet, having been by-passed by the main road to the coast. At the western end is the completely restored **Wordsworth House and Garden** (mid-Mar–Oct Sat–Thu 11am–5pm), where the poet was born in 1770, now owned by the National Trust. Wordsworth's father was steward to

Actors help Wordsworth House to remain firmly in the past.

the great landowning Lonsdale family. The house is furnished in the original style and great care has been taken in bringing it back to the condition it was in during Wordsworth's time. Some of the poet's personal effects are on display, and actors in period costume play the parts of the servants, cooking, cleaning and working in the garden.

A memorial window to Wordsworth is to be found in **All Saints' Church**, a Victorian structure boasting a 180ft (55m) spire and no fewer than eight bells in the belfry.

Close to the castle (see box) is **Jennings Brewery**. Established over 175 years ago, the company moved to Cockermouth in 1874. Their Castle Brewery runs guided tours (www. jenningsbrewery.co.uk;   Feb–Mar, Nov–Dec Mon–Fri 2pm, Sat noon, 2pm, Apr–Oct Mon–Sat noon, 2pm), where you see beer being made and try their Sneck Lifter, Cocker Hoop and other ales, including seasonal ales such as Bloomin' Marvellous, Pigs Might Fly and Cockle Warmer.

COASTAL TOWNS

You might like to take a detour from Cockermouth to explore the nearby coast. If so, continue on westwards on the A66 to Workington and then up the A596 to Maryport. Bus X4/X5 carries on to Workington, from where you can take the train north to Maryport and south to Whitehaven.

Several villages in the Cockermouth area have produced famous historical figures. Amongst them is Fletcher Christian, who mutinied on the *Bounty*, and who was born at Moorland Close in 1764. John Dalton of atomic theory fame was born in Eaglesfield in 1766. Fearon Fallows was born in Cockermouth in 1789 was Astronomer Royal to George IV.

Cockermouth Castle

This stronghold was built in the 12th century to repulse Scottish raiders. It was involved in the 15th-century War of the Roses, and in 1648 during the Civil War it held out for Parliament. The castle has suffered more from decay than from warlike forces. One wing, rebuilt in the 19th century, is privately occupied. The castle is open to the public only on special occasions, usually during the Cockermouth Festival in June/July.

Now mostly a romantic ruin, the castle has a feisty past.

A port since Roman times, Maryport was developed into a coal port in the 18th century and is a fine example of a Georgian planned town.

On the coast, from north to south, the harbour at **Maryport ❺** has been restored, and, in the attendant **Maritime Museum** (www.maryportmaritimemuseum.btck.co.uk; Apr–Oct Tue, Thu–Sun 10am–5pm, Nov–Mar Fri–Sun 10.30am–4pm), you'll learn about the local seagoing traditions, as well as the life of Fletcher Christian. A Great War Exhibition will be on display until 2018. Don't miss the cliff-top **Senhouse Roman Museum** (www.senhousemuseum.co.uk; Apr–Oct daily 10am–5pm; Nov–Mar Fri–Sun 10.30am–4pm), with artefacts from the excavations at a nearby fort.

In **Workington ❻**, the next town down the coast, the **Helena Thompson Museum** has displays charting its maritime and social history (www.helenathompson.org.uk; Sun–Wed 1.30–4.30pm; free). **Workington Hall** (currently closed to the public) in Curwen Park – refuge for Mary, Queen of Scots during her last night of freedom in May 1568 – is a ruin, but plaques give visitors a flavour of the hall's long history, dating from the

14th century, when it was simply a pele tower.

To the south on the A595 is **Whitehaven ❼**, a stimulating town with a red-stone promontory and some excellent museums. It's also near **St Bees Head**, Cumbria's most westerly point, and starting point of Wainwright's 190-mile (306km) Coast to Coast Walk across northern England.

Whitehaven's role in the rum trade unfolds at **The Rum Story** (www.rumstory.co.uk; daily 10am–4.30pm; www.rumstory.co.uk), set in the Jefferson family's 18th-century premises. Delve further into the area's history at **The Beacon** (www.thebeacon-whitehaven.co.uk; Tue–Sun 10am–4.30pm), where interactive exhibits and galleries are spread across five floors. A footpath leads from behind The Beacon to **Haig Pit Colliery Mining Museum** (www.haigpit.co.uk; Tue–Sun 10am–4pm, also Mon during school hols) on the former site of the Haig Pit. The museum, reopened in 2015 following restoration work, evokes the lives of miners and the traditions of the West

Cumbria coalfields. There is a visitor centre, café and shop on the site.

THORNTHWAITE FOREST

Another side trip from Cockermouth is to **Loweswater** ❽ ('leafy lake'), a tranquil spot with a pleasant lakeside walk, by road on the B5289 south. Or phone the Dial-a-Ride service in Cockermouth (tel: 01900-822795) the day before to check if bus No. 949 is running to Lorton and Buttermere. The road runs through Lorton Vale to the village of Loweswater at the southeastern end of the lake, which is almost shadowed by **Mellbreak** (1,676ft/511m). Clinker-built rowing boats can be hired here from the National Trust Watergate Farm. Carry on to Buttermere village and back to enjoy fine views of **Crummock Water**.

From Buttermere you can pick up the 77A that runs back up to High Lorton and then turns right on the B5292 over the **Whinlatter Pass** ❾, passing through Thornthwaite Forest where a **Visitor Centre** (daily 10am–4pm) has details of various trails and cycle routes, and live video feeds of red squirrels and the ospreys on **Bassenthwaite**

Lake. The lake can be seen from a vantage point by the road that also has a good-weather view of Skiddaw. The centre offers the Go Ape! (www.go.ape.co.uk; 0333-3317293; book in advance) adventure course with zip slides, rope bridges and the new Go Ape Forest Segway adventure. Bassenthwaite Lake is 4 miles (6km) long, half a mile (0.8km) wide and 51ft (16m) deep. There is a sailing club here, but no settlement. The A66 to and from the towns of the west Cumbrian coast runs along the west side of the lake.

White Bishop

Beside the A66 on the southwest side of Bassenthwaite is the former Swan Hotel. In a wooded area nearby, on the old road through Braithwaite and Thornthwaite, is the hill known as Barf (the pronunciation of Barugh, a north-country surname). A tradition in the hotel was to reward with a pint of beer a volunteer who whitewashed the large stone called the Bishop of Barf. This was the place where a man who fancied himself as a skilled horseman came to grief when attempting to ride up that side of the mountain. Today the pub no longer operates, and the stone is kept white by Keswick Mountain Res-

Bridge crossing over Bassenthwaite Lake.

Bassenthwaite Ospreys

After an absence of many years, in 2001 a pair of ospreys made a nest on Bassenthwaite Lake. They returned in subsequent years, after wintering in Africa, and raised several chicks. Returning for a third year in 2015, descendants of those original birds produced two chicks. In the summer the birds can usually be seen from the viewpoint at Dodd Wood, where telescopes have been set up (for more information see www.ospreywatch.co.uk).

At a distance the fish-eating osprey is often mistaken for a seagull.

cue Team. The way the horseman took is mainly scree – a safer path approaches the summit from the side and back.

Mirehouse

About 3.5 miles (5.5km) above Keswick, on the east side of the lake, is **Mirehouse** ❿ (www.mirehouse.co. uk; house: Apr–Oct Wed, Sat–Sun 1.30–4.30pm, also Fri in Aug; gardens: Apr–Oct daily 10am–5pm), reached by bus 73 or 73A dependent on direction of travel. The large family home, built in 1666, was extended in 1790 with a stylish porch of red sandstone. There is a Poets' Walk in the garden – the Sped-

Mirehouse, where Tennyson stayed and wrote 'Morte d'Arthur'.

ding family who lived here were friends with Wordsworth, Tennyson, Southey, Thomas Carlyle and the painter John Constable. Children are welcome, and there is an owl hunt for the younger age group and a history quiz for older ones. There is a good tearoom opposite the entrance, and you can also stroll to the edge of Bassenthwaite Lake and look around **St Bega's**, an ancient church restored in Victorian times.

Crosthwaite Church

Before entering the town, visit **Crosthwaite Church** ⓫, on the northern edge of Keswick, where the gateway is adorned by Celtic motifs designed by Canon Rawnsley (1851–1920), a former vicar and local literary figure. The first church would have been made of wood and thatch, but traces of the stone Norman building that succeeded it are to be found in the north-aisle wall of the present church. In 1844 it was completely restored under the direction of Sir George Gilbert Scott. Look for the marble figure of Robert Southey (1774–1843), who worshipped here for 40 years. His memorial, written by Wordsworth, is in the southeast corner of the church, and his grave is on the north side.

Crosthwaite Church.

Eating Out

Cockermouth
The Honest Lawyer
2 Main Street; tel: 01900-824888;
www.honestlawyerrestaurant.co.uk;
Tue–Sat noon–2.30pm, 5–9.30pm,
Sun noon–3.30pm.
Dishes featuring local produce,
including tasty rump of lamb and
pan-fried wood pigeon, are on the
menu here. Vegetarians are well
catered for, too. ££

The Quince and Medlar
13 Castlegate; tel: 01900-823579;
www.quinceandmedlar.co.uk; Tue–Sat
7–10.30pm.
This attractive vegetarian spot cooks
up excellent, inventive food with
fresh, local ingredients. Good wine
list. ££

Whitehaven
Zest Harbourside
8 West Strand; tel: 01946-66981;
www.zestwhitehaven.com; daily
11.45am–9pm (Fri–Sat until 9.30pm).
The Harbourside is a fun bar, which
serves up a wide range of dishes,
from home-made burgers to stir-fried
pork. £

Zest Restaurant
Low Road; tel: 01946-692848; as
above; Wed–Sat 6.30–9.30pm (Sat
until 10pm).

Grilled meats, particularly steak,
feature heavily at the more upmarket
partner to the Harbourside. ££

Bassenthwaite
Bistro at the Distillery
Setmurthy; tel: 017687-88852;
www.bistroatthedistillery.com; daily
11am–9pm.
Not far from the northern shores of
the lake, the bistro is located at the
award-winning Lakes Distillery. Good
honest cooking using Cumbrian
produce and some interesting
desserts. ££

Mirehouse
The Old Sawmill Tearoom
Mirehouse; tel: 017687-74317;
www.mirehouse.co.uk; daily 10am–
5.30pm, check for winter opening.
Overlooking the lake, this café serves
a range of cakes and light meals. £

The Pheasant
Bassenthwaite Lake; tel: 017687-
76234; www.the-pheasant.co.uk; daily
noon–4.30pm, 6–9pm; restaurant:
Sun lunch, Tue–Sat dinner 7–9pm,
booking advised.
A laid-back bistro and fine-dining
restaurant are found at this
traditional old inn. Try the wild
salmon or 28-day sirloin steak, and
inventive desserts. ££

Wildlife

Raptors soar overhead, deer prance through the woods where red squirrels chatter, while voles and otters steal through the clear waters. There's plenty to watch out for

Despite high visitor traffic, the Lakes remain an important habitat for a large number of animals and birds, which are an extra reason to pack a pair of binoculars in your rucksack.

MAMMALS

The water in some of the tarns and lakes is so pure and algae-free that mammals have little to eat, but you may be lucky enough to see an otter gliding by. Among smaller mammals are the water voles and water shrews that live in the stony brooks. Other small animals include the common doormouse, which survives in Dud-

don Valley and Grizedale.

For years, the Lake District has been a stronghold of the red squirrel. Although endangered, it is still hanging on in Dodd Wood near Keswick and Greystoke Forest near Penrith.

The largest of Britain's land mammals, the red deer, can be seen at Martindale, a secluded valley beyond Howtown near Ullswater. Smaller roe deer are widespread, and new plantations have to be fenced against them.

The red fox is common, benefiting from the ban on hunting with dogs, and badgers are also found, mainly in pockets of old deciduous woodland.

There is a good chance you'll spot a peregrine falcon.

Wildlife Spotting

The following locations are a selection of the best to visit for a chance of seeing some of the wonderful animals that inhabit the Lakes.

Dodd Wood: You stand a good chance of seeing red squirrels, as well as, in summer, getting a view of the ospreys on Bassenthwaite Lake.

Grizedale Forest: This large tract of woodland in southern Lakeland is home to common doormice and red deer, as well as large numbers of woodland birds.

Martindale: This estate between Ullswater and Haweswater is home to herds of red deer. You might catch a glimpse of the magnificent animals from a cruise on the lake.

St Bees Head: The cliffs here have large colonies of guillemots, herring gulls, kittiwakes, razorbills and fulmars.

Whinlatter Forest Park: England's only mountain forest is the place to see red squirrels, and you can watch the Bassenthwaite ospreys on a large screen – the birds usually arrive in late March.

On the hills you may encounter wild fell ponies, which were once used to carry minerals for the mining industry.

BIRDS

The region is famed for its cliff-nesting species, although the only golden eagle in England, resident at Riggindale, still has to find a mate. Peregrine falcons, ravens and buzzards, which nest in fell country, are relatively common. Ospreys, which first nested by Bassenthwaite Lake in 2001 – the first in the English wild for over 150 years – continue to return each year and successfully raise chicks.

Pied flycatchers, nuthatches, wood warblers, tree pipits and the three varieties of woodpeckers are well suited to the mature woodlands. Canada geese are frequently seen around Grasmere. Greylag geese are locally common by Derwent Water and Coniston Water.

On the coast, St Bees Head has one of England's largest nesting colonies of sea birds.

Wast Water is the least changed of the lakes.

The Western Lakes

Starting from Ambleside, this 60-mile (97km) tour heads off into some spectacular scenery, from the Langdale Pikes to Wast Water

The western Lake District is out of the way, and public transport scarce, but it is well worth the effort of making the journey. One of the truly great sights is the Screes beyond Wast Water, preferably lit by a setting sun, draped like giant fans from a 1,700ft (518m) long cliff, the south-eastern buttress of sprawling Scafell. Elsewhere, the prominent features are stern and offer bottomless solitude.

LANGDALE VALLEY

Begin in Ambleside, and head westwards on the A593. If using public transport, you can catch the No. 516 bus (daily Easter–Oct) from Kelsick Road to Dungeon Ghyll. The road, in its meanderings, offers glimpses

Highlights

- Skelwith Force
- The Langdale Pikes
- The Wrynose and Hardknott Passes
- The Ravenglass and Eskdale Railway
- Wasdale and Wast Water
- Great Gable and Scafell Pike
- Ennerdale

of the **River Brathay**, Norse for a broad river, which gathers up near the Three Shires Stone on Wrynose Pass and has transfusions of cold beck water from Little Langdale before presenting a white-water spectacle near **Skelwith Bridge**. Near Loughrigg

most distinctive landforms in the district. Elterwater has a common, which is a grazing area for Herdwicks. The evidence of slate quarrying is everywhere, and a terrace of slate dwellings overlooking the common is particularly attractive. There are few visible remains of the old gunpowder factory that supplied the quarries. In its place is a large residential complex.

Great Langdale

Great Langdale doesn't have a lake, but it has all the other attributes of a picturesque Lakeland valley – a beck, green fields hatched by dry-stone walls, and mountains blocking out more than half the sky. The passes of Wrynose and Hardknott are not for the timid, especially on a bicycle, but they make a spectacular 'valley' walk.

Great Langdale proper is entered from the pretty village of **Chapel Stile**, in which the most prominent building is **Holy Trinity Church**. The church stands on a hill as though on a ledge, which means that church-going requires physical as well as spiritual stamina. In the churchyard is the grave of G.M. Trevelyan, author of the classic *English Social History*, published in 1944.

Walking in the Langdale Valley.

Tarn it is a short walk to **Skelwith Force ❶** ('the noisy fall') which, though only 15ft high (4.5m) high, is a cheerful sight.

From Skelwith Bridge the bus heads for Great Langdale, which bursts into view near **Elterwater**. Across the common and beyond the woodland rise the **Langdale Pikes**, among the

Prehistoric Industry

Just below Pike o' Stickle is one of the most important prehistoric sites in the country. The outcrop of hard Lakeland greenstone above the scree was the location for a stone axe factory in Neolithic times (4000–2000 BC). Finds made from the stone have been discovered as far afield as Ireland and Lincolnshire. Amongst the debris of the screes it is still possible to see 'rejected' bits of stone that have been half worked.

Pike o'Stickle, whose stone was honed into Neolithic axe blades.

Pike o' Stickle.

Beyond the village of Chapel Stile, Thrang Crag and the residues of slate quarrying are prominent, as is a terrace of houses and flats. It is unwise to explore redundant quarries without taking local advice and wearing a stout helmet.

The bus finishes its journey by the Old Dungeon Ghyll Hotel, the haunt of generations of walkers and climbers. Dungeon Ghyll enters the valley from the northwest. Walk a little way up the beck to see the impressive

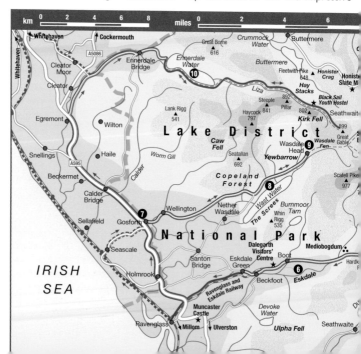

60ft (18m) waterfall of **Dungeon Ghyll Force** ❷.

Back down in the valley, the Langdale Pikes dominate the valley with the mighty impact of a Sphinx. The three fells that can be seen are **Harrison Stickle** (the highest, at 2,414ft/736m), **Pike o' Stickle** and **Pavey Ark**, though there are actually five summits in the group. The Pikes can be ascended, granted with some effort, from the New Dungeon Ghyll Hotel. Near the foot of Pavey Ark's 600ft (183m) cliff lies **Stickle Tarn,** which, dammed in 1824, provided a constant head of water, via the river, for the gunpowder works down at the village of Elterwater.

A great scramble, Jack's Rake, leads diagonally across the face of Pavey Ark up to the summit at 2,288ft (697m). This gives fantastic views, but also quite a degree of exposure, and is only for the experienced climber.

The '**Langdale Round**', starting from the ascent of Pavey Ark, is one of the finest outings on the fells. This 13-mile (21km) walk takes you over Harrison Stickle and around the head of the valley by Angle Tarn and up Bow Fell (2,960ft/902m).

In good weather the view from Bow Fell over to Scafell is stupendous. From Bow Fell you either descend into the side valley of Oxendale, or carry on to the peak of Pike o' Blisco (2,304ft/702m), from where you can make your way back to Dungeon Ghyll.

Blea Tarn

A road leaves the valley heading south near **Wall End Farm** – notice the large boulders in and beside the beck – and climbs to **Blea Tarn** ❸. This is in a secluded little valley, where an attractive farmhouse was the home of Solitary, a character who appears in one of Wordsworth's poems. The tarn is surrounded by trees and a grove of rhododendrons.

Beneath the Langdale Pikes is Blea Tarn. It's easy to reach and contains brown trout, perch and pike.

THE WRYNOSE AND HARDKNOTT PASSES

The road from Blea Tarn joins the road westwards over the Wrynose and Hardknott Passes. There is no scheduled bus service that runs this way, but you might want to check out one of the Mountain Goat tours ('High Adventure Tour'; www.mountain-goat.co.uk; Mar–Oct daily, Nov–Feb depending on weather), which heads over the passes and down to the railway in Eskdale, and then over to Wast Water and on to Coniston and through the Yewdale Valley after a visit to Muncaster Castle.

The **Wrynose Pass ❹** is sometimes referred to as the 'pass of the stallion', the implication being that a strong horse was needed to negotiate it. Wrynose has a steep gradient, taking little time to attain 1,289ft (393m), and a good surface, which is the result of work carried out after World War II, when it was used for military training.

The road descends to the head of the **Duddon Valley**, where **Hardknott Pass** 5 (more fearsome than Wrynose) begins its course to Esk-

dale with a steep gradient and a quick succession of hairpin bends, delivering the motorist to an elevation of 1,291ft (393m). Care is needed during the descent. Beside the road, on a plateau looking into Eskdale, are the considerable remains of **Mediobogdum**, a Roman fort. Wordsworth, in one of his sonnets about the River Duddon, pictured an eagle flying over the ruins of a fort 'whose guardians bent the knee to Jove and Mars'.

At the summit of Wrynose is a stone pillar marked 'Lancashire' but generally known as Three Shires Stone. Here, before local government reorganisation in 1974, the counties of Cumberland, Westmorland and Lancashire met.

ESKDALE

Lakeless **Eskdale** 6 extends down to **Boot**. Just beyond the village of Eskdale Green is a station for the **Ravenglass and Eskdale Railway** (www.ravenglass-railway.co.uk; late Mar–Oct daily, Nov–mid-Mar services some weekends), affectionately known as 'Ratty'. This is England's oldest narrow-gauge steam railway, opened in 1875 to carry iron ore down to the coast for shipping, and operated, with a few breaks, until 1960 when it was taken over by a group of enthusiasts determined to preserve the line.

The railway runs for 7 miles (11km) from the visitors' centre at **Dalegarth**, down to **Ravenglass** harbour, where the story of the Railway is told in the Railway Museum. The journey takes 40 minutes each way. On the way down to the coast you will pass **Muncaster Water Mill**. Privately owned and not open to the public, it dates from the mid-15th century. To the south, close to the A595 is the 14th-century **Muncaster Castle** (www.muncaster.co.uk; castle Apr–Oct Sun–Fri noon–4.30pm, gardens, Owl Centre and maze mid-Feb–Dec daily 10.30am–5pm, shorter

Easy enough by car today, but Wrynose Pass once required a strong horse to negotiate its rugged terrain.

The Ravenglass and Eskdale Railway has been running since 1875.

hours in winter), a supposedly haunted castle still lived in as a family home. In the stunning gardens, complete with Europe's largest collection of rhododendrons, is the World Owl Centre with a fascinating array of birds.

Ravenglass was an important Roman naval base, Glannaventa, in the 2nd century, as it lies on the estuary of three rivers, the Esk, the Mite and the Irt. It also marks the west end of Hadrian's Wall. Little remains of the town, except a large bath house, now known as Walls Castle. This is one of the largest remaining Roman structures in England, about 40ft (12m) by 90ft (27m) and with walls over 12ft (3.5m) high, and would have contained all a Roman's bathing needs, from hot saunas to cold plunges.

If going from Eskdale to Ravenglass by car, take the road westwards to Gubbergill to join the A595. Turn right for Ravenglass. The town can also be reached on the railway via Ulverston and Milom. There is no public transport to reach Wasdale and Wast Waster, although those using the coastal railway could take the train from Ravenglass to Seascale and cycle via Gosforth.

Getting Around

It is not possible to do this route completely by public transport, and to take in most of the sights you might want to call on the services of Mountain Goat (see page 92). The Ravenglass and Eskdale Railway provides a great way to get around, while buses between Ambleside and Langdale are regular. To see Wasdale and Ennerdale without a car, you might be better off taking your bike on the railway (pre-book) and cycling from the coast.

Ravenglass railway station on the Ravenglass and Eskdale line.

Viking Cross

Continuing the drive, take the A595 north to **Gosforth** ❼ to see the 14.5ft (4.5m) carved **Viking Cross** in the churchyard at St Mary's. Made of red sandstone, and somewhat worn after nine centuries of wind and rain, the cross was raised when paganism was giving way to Christianity. Images from Norse mythology and Christian symbolism are portrayed.

Turn right towards Wellington.

WASDALE

On the journey through Wasdale, there is a view of **Wast Water** ❽ that has been voted Britain's favourite view. Cold and blue, Wast Water is the least changed of the great lakes, since they were formed by the scouring of glacial ice. It is also the deepest in England, reaching 260ft (79m), and in places it extends more than 50ft (15m) below sea level. The famous **Screes** are part of a 3-mile (5km) cliff on a fell known as Illgill Head (1,998ft/609m).

The clear waters of Wast Water, looking towards Wasdale Head.

The road, in places unfenced, stays close to the northern shore of the lake and is fringed by sheep-cropped vegetation and gorse, which turns the landscape yellow in spring.

The glorious scenery unfolds slowly as the journey proceeds. On the left is **Yewbarrow**, which is not much

A stunning sunset drapes Wast Water in shades of orange and red.

Climbing Scafell Pike

The most direct way to climb England's highest mountain, Scafell Pike (3,209ft/978m), is from the northern end of Wast Water. Take the path that leads up Lingmell Gill, climbing steeply below the crags overhead. This will, eventually, bring you out directly at the summit, with wonderful views all around. An alternative, although more serious, ending to the route is the scramble up through the screes of Mickledore.

Telephone box on a remote lane.

higher than 2,000ft (610m) but has a 'mountain' appearance. It is a long drag over grassy terrain to reach the summit, which is a vantage point for the really big fells of the dalehead. However, they can also be seen and admired from the road.

At centre stage and standing at 2,949ft (899m), **Great Gable** is a rugged pyramid that looks like a child's drawing of a mountain (see page 73). Its companions are **Kirk Fell**

(2,360ft/719m), **Broad Crag** and **Scafell Pike** (3,209ft/978m). From the floor of Wasdale Valley, Great Gable actually seems larger than Scafell Pike, England's highest peak.

Tall stories

Unlike most dales, **Wasdale Head** ❾ does not get narrower and rockier as it comes to its head. For here is a great tract of alluvial soil, thatched in lush green, overlaid by an intricate and fascinating pattern of dry-stone walls. Over the centuries so much stone has been cleared from the land that a lot was simply heaped up and walled around.

The **Wasdale Head Inn** has rooms and apartments decked with photographs of early climbers. The Ritson Bar is named after Will Ritson, an archetypal dalesman who told 'tall' stories and was fond of saying that Wasdale had the biggest mountain, the deepest lake and the biggest liar – himself (see page 65).

Tiny church

The **church** at Wasdale Head, one of the smallest in England, has timbers salvaged from a shipwrecked vessel. On a window the outline of **Napes Needle**, Great Gable's celebrated

Hay Stacks, in the vicinity of Great Gable, was much loved by Alfred Wainwright, who chose it as the place where he wanted his ashes scattered.

rock pinnacle, has been scratched. A conquest of the Needle is obligatory in the career of a Lake District climber. To this end Wasdale attracted a host of Victorian climbers, some of whom would first practise on the gable end of a local barn.

The first ascent of the Napes Needle, by Walter Parry Haskett Smith in 1886, marked the beginning of rock climbing as a sport, rather than simply as part of general mountain hiking. The classic route, put up by Smith, follows a fizzure to the summit and an-

Pillar and Kirk Fell are spectacular in all seasons.

other one climbs up the ledge. The view from the top is amazing.

Shapely fells

Wasdale, its Screes and the dalehead with the pyramid of Great Gable all lie at the centre of a trinity of shapely fells. Most people are captivated – but not Wordsworth, who described Wast Water as 'long, narrow, stern and desolate'. Coleridge, in 1802, infused plenty of life and colour into his description of the Screes as 'consisting of fine red Streaks running in broad Stripes thro' a stone colour – slanting off from the Perpendicular, as steep as the meal newly ground from the Miller's Spout…like a pointed Decanter in shape, or an outspread fan.'

On to Ennerdale

If it was tricky getting to Wasdale, the final section of this route is even more difficult without your own transport. By car, you'll need to drive back to Gosforth and take the A595 north to Egremont. Here, take the road heading northwest to Ennerdale Bridge.

Public transport is minimal to Ennerdale Water, as the area is remote, and the only bus is No. 217 (Frizington–Cockermouth route), which calls at Ennerdale Bridge but only twice a day on a Wednesday.

ENNERDALE

Just before the modern village of **Ennerdale Bridge**, a stone circle to the right on the moor is, in fact, a Victorian folly.

From Ennerdale Bridge the road continues a short way to **Ennerdale Water ❿** but there is no road around the lake. This is the most westerly of the lakes and one of the most remote. It is 2.5 miles (4km) long, and walkers on the Coast to Coast route, or day-trippers with plenty of time and energy, walk to the head of Ennerdale. Most of the shore is owned by the National Trust, but the forest surrounding the lake, one of the largest in Cumbria, is managed by the Forestry Commission, who have planted many conifers. The lake acts as a reservoir for the coastal towns, and is exceptionally clear.

As the backwoods are left behind, the towering peaks of Great Gable, Kirk Fell, Pillar and Steeple come into view with Hay Stacks rising behind a remote and solitary building, **Black Sail** youth hostel, which is only accessible by foot.

Eating Out

Langdale
The Hikers Bar
Old Dungeon Ghyll Hotel; tel: 015394-37272; www.odg.co.uk; daily noon–2pm, 6–9pm.
This famed bar, with its cosy nooks, has honest and filling pub food, just right after a day on the fells. £
The New Dungeon Ghyll Hotel
Great Langdale; tel: 015394-37 213; www.dungeon-ghyll.co.uk; Walkers' Bar 8am–9pm, restaurant 6–8.30pm.
The food at the namesake of the longer-established hotel is a good mix of modern European dishes (restaurant) and hearty British grub (bar). £ (bar), ££ (restaurant)

Eskdale
The Boot Inn
Boot; tel: 01946-723711; www.thebooteskdale.co.uk; Sun noon–7pm, Mon 5–8pm, Tue–Thu noon–8pm, Fri–Sat noon–9pm.
Well placed for Scafell Pike and the Ravenglass Railway, this place has plenty of choice on its menu, from lamb shank to curry of the day. ££
The Brook House Inn
Boot; tel: 01946-723288; www.brook house.inn; daily lunch and dinner.
The excellent range of local beers here is backed up by good pub food. The fish is especially tasty. ££
Turntable Café and Fellbites
Ravenglass and Dalegarth respectively; tel: 01229-717171; www.ravenglass-railway.co.uk; Mar–Nov daily 9.30am–4.30pm, varies according to timetables.
These two cafés (at either end of the Ravenglass and Eskdale Railway) offer meals as well as home-baked cakes. £

Wasdale
Gosforth Hall Inn
Gosforth; tel: 019467-25322; www.gosforthhall.co.uk; food served: Mon–Sat 4–8.30pm.
If you are very hungry, the legendary home-made pies here should do the trick. There are also lighter dishes, such as fillet of fish of the day. ££
The Wasdale Head Inn
Wasdale Head; tel: 019467-26229; www.wasdale.com; daily noon–8pm.
Open 365 days a year, this inn offers good beer, fine views and hearty food such as Herdwick lamb. ££

Morecambe Bay.

Tour 8

The Southwest

Numerous attractions lie around the southern coast, and this 66-mile (106km) tour starting at Grange-over-Sands covers a great variety, from stately homes to an aquarium

The tide sweeps across Morecambe Bay with the speed of a good horse. It performs pincer movements round the sand bars and spreads itself languidly over the mudflats. In a short time, what had been a damp desert is an arm of the sea, choppy and chilling. Then, with another turn of the tide, the bay is once again what someone called a 'wet Sahara', though this is no desert.

On the mudbanks thrive small creatures that sustain dense flocks of wintering birds. Years ago, the bay at low tide would be alive with village fisherfolk, who, with horses and carts and tackle, sought cockles, mussels, dabs, flukes and Morecambe Bay shrimps. People still fish and forage here, but the bay is tinged with the disaster of

Highlights

- Grange-over-Sands
- Cartmel
- Holker Hall
- Ulverston
- Dalton-in-Furness
- Furness Abbey
- The Duddon Valley
- Grizedale Forest
- The Lakes Aquarium

2004, when 21 unsuspecting Chinese cocklepickers were drowned, cut off by the tide.

North of the bay are limestone hills and, beyond, the high fells, and a journey in this area is ever-varied. From Grange-over-Sands – a good starting point served by rail and bus – this route runs through Furness, up into the glorious Duddon Valley. It then retraces its steps to explore Grizedale Forest, ending up by Lakeside at the southern end of Lake Windermere.

GRANGE-OVER-SANDS

On the coastal railway route that splits off from the West Coast Main Line at Carnforth, **Grange-over-Sands ❶** began as a monastic 'grange' or granary. The fishing village developed when it was connected to the rail network in 1857, and tourists arrived. In Victorian and Edwardian times wealthy

merchants constructed grand houses here, some of which are now hotels. But the lack of a proper seaside beach prevented it from becoming a full-blown resort. Today, with a formal park and lake, elegant shops with cast-iron canopies, and the cosy retro promenade tearoom, it remains a quiet, sedate seaside town.

A two-hour circular walk leads from the town through woodland and open fell to **Hampsfell**. Here a restored shelter-cum-observation point offers fine-weather views, taking in Ingleborough and other Yorkshire peaks as well as those of the Lake District.

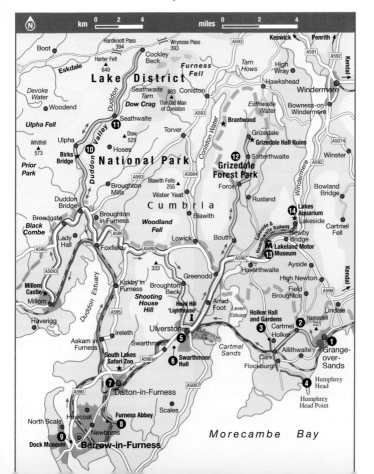

A quiet morning in Cartmel.

CARTMEL

Take bus No. 532 (Mon–Fri only) from Grange-over-Sands railway station to **Cartmel ❷**. As the village comes into view, you will be able to

Holker Hall, complete with its award-wining garden, has been in the Cavendish family hands for 400 years.

admire the preserved **Priory** (www.cartmelpriory.org.uk; daily 9am–5.30pm (3.30pm in winter); free), described by Simon Jenkins in *England's Thousand Best Churches* as 'the most beautiful church in the north-west'. Dating from 1188, its magnificent interior includes medieval stained glass and beautifully carved misericords and choir stalls.

The 14th-century **monastic gatehouse**, which was in use from 1624 until 1790 as a grammar school, is the only other surviving part of the original monastery and it now belongs to the National Trust. Cartmel Village Shop is home of the famous Cartmel Sticky Toffee Pudding (www.cartmel villageshop.co.uk), and it sells a wide range of other local produce.

Anyone who likes a flutter might like to visit the small Cartmel Racecourse, with its lovely setting and old-style social gathering.

HOLKER HALL

The No. 532 goes on to the railway station at **Cark**, where a weath-

Cartmel Priory.

ervane on the church is a gilded fish, a measure of how important fishing was here. Just beyond Cark is **Holker Hall** ❸ (www.holker.co.uk; Apr–Oct, Wed–Sun hall: 11am–4pm, gardens, café, food hall and shop: 10.30am–5pm; café, food hall and shop also open Nov–20 Dec Fri–Sun). The splendid home of the Cavendish family dates from 1871, replacing a previous building gutted by fire.

Red sandstone was used to create a building that has a markedly Elizabethan style, though part of the old 17th-century house remains. It was the home of the Preston family, benefactors of Cartmel Priory, though the Cavendishes have been here for over 400 years. The Long Gallery, where the Victorian architects drew on an Elizabethan idea, is beautifully finished, while the wooden staircase shows off the great skill of the workers who rebuilt the hall.

Holker is set in an award-winning garden, which, in turn, lies within a deer-haunted park. Joseph Paxton, designer of the Crystal Palace, was invited to plant the 'monkey puzzle tree' (Chilean pine) that has now reached such an enormous size that it has to be pinned to stop it falling over. The venerable Holker Lime, listed as one of 50 Great British Trees, is here, and there are a number of rare plants, including the national collection of Styracaceae. Holker Hall is the venue for a notable annual garden festival (see the website for details).

The Courtyard Café at Holker Hall serves local food.

Holker Food Hall

Holker Hall's farm shop is one of the best places in the Lakes to buy local produce. Among the foodstuffs they stock are Holker saltmarsh lamb from their 15,000-acre (6,070ha) estate, game in season, local beers and damson gin. Their selection of cheeses is particularly good, especially those made by Holker Farm Dairy. Holker Food Hall (www.holker.co.uk; Apr–Oct Wed–Sun 10.30am–5pm and Nov–20 Dec Fri–Sun).

Cycling up Harlock Hill, near Ulverston.

Flookburgh and Humphrey Head

Staying on the No. 532 beyond Cark will bring you to **Flookburgh**. A mile or so inland from Morecambe Bay, Flookburgh was a village of horse-and-cart fisherfolk, who operated on the bay at low tide. Shrimps were caught by a trawl net with a beam that scooped the shrimps into the net.

Morecambe Bay shrimps: small, brown and terribly tasty.

Cockles by the ton were once transported in sacks from here via the railway station at Cark.

The promontory to the south of Flookburgh is **Humphrey Head** ❹, the highest point on the west coast between Wales and St Bees Head.

ULVERSTON

Return to Cark and drive or take the train to Ulverston, passing through an almost flat landscape that consists of sappy grass and indigenous woodland, where wildlife flourishes. The railway crosses over the **Leven Estuary**, where the outflow from Windermere mixes with the salty tide. On the other, western, side of the bridge is **Ulverston** ❺, which has a distinctly nautical flavour. The ship canal from the bay was built by John Rennie in 1796, but is now in effect a static water tank for the Glaxo-Smith-Kline pharmaceutical company. Ulverston has become widely known for its **Laurel and Hardy Museum** (daily 10am–5pm (closed Mon and Wed Nov–Easter); www.laurel-and-hardy.co.uk), based at the Roxy Cinema on Brogden

George Romney

The English portrait painter George Romney (1734–1802) was born in Dalton-in-Furness and studied painting in Kendal (you can still see a number of his works in the gallery there; see page 16). He is particularly known for his series of paintings of Lady Emma Hamilton, mistress of Lord Nelson. During his time he was one of the most successful of society portrait painters, even rivalling Sir Joshua Reynolds.

Emma, Lady Hamilton, as Bacchante, a typical pose for Romney.

Street. Stan Laurel was born in the town in 1890, and as well as telling the story of the silent movie comedy duo's lives, the museum has regular showings of their films.

Hoad Hill 'Lighthouse'

The limestone 'lighthouse' on Hoad Hill in Ulverston is a scaled-down model of the Eddystone lighthouse, built in 1850 in memory of the naval administrator and traveller Sir John Barrow (1764–1848), a native of the town and founder of the Royal Geographical Society. Hoad Hill may be climbed from Ulverston in under half an hour.

SWARTHMOOR

Take the A590, bus 6/X6 (Mon–Fri only) or walk for 15 minutes from Ulverston station to reach **Swarthmoor Hall ⑥** (www.swarthmoor hall.co.uk; Mar–Oct Mon–Fri 10.30–4.30pm, Sun and last Thu of each month opens at 1.30pm; audio tours available), an Elizabethan building of major interest to Quakers. George Fox, founder of the Society of Friends, was a frequent visitor from 1652, when the hall was owned by Judge Thomas Fell and his wife, Margaret. When the judge died in 1658, the immunity he had secured for Quakers lapsed, and they were persecuted. Margaret later married George Fox, and both suffered hardship and imprisonment for their beliefs. The hall is still owned by the Religious Society of Friends (the Quakers), who run residential and day courses here.

Hoad Hill lighthouse, one of Cumbria's best-known landmarks.

Furness Abbey, one of the richest monastic institutions in England until the Reformation, is now a ruin, but it still manages to impress.

DALTON-IN-FURNESS

Turn left on the A590 or continue on the train or bus to the small town of **Dalton-in-Furness** ❼, the birthplace of the painter George Romney (see box). The town's **castle** (www.nationaltrust.org.uk; Apr–Sept Sat 2–5pm; free) is an attractive, square 14th-century building in the town's main street. It was built by the Abbot of Furness Abbey when Scottish raiders were troublesome, and some of the Abbey's attractive red sandstone was used to repair the tower after the monastery was dissolved. The building became a prison and courthouse, and the two-storey 'castle' now contains a small exhibition on the history of the town, and of George Romney.

Dalton had its economic heyday in the 19th century with the growth of ironstone mining and the lifting of 7 million tons of ore from local mines. Today, the town is more widely known for the **South Lakes Safari Zoo** (www.southlakessafarizoo.com; daily Easter–Oct 10am–5pm, Nov–Easter 10am–4.30pm, Aug until 6pm). One of the best conservation zoos in the country, it underwent major expansion in 2014. Species on show range from free-flying parrots to Sumatran tigers, and pygmy hippos to red-eared terrapins. Buses 6/X6 stop at the zoo's boundary.

FURNESS ABBEY

Not far from Dalton, between the stations of Dalton Castle and Roose, a small road leads under a monastic arch to the superb remains of **Furness Abbey** ❽ (Apr–Sept daily 10am–6pm, Oct 10am–5pm, Nov–Mar Sat–Sun 10am–4pm), administered by English Heritage. Founded in 1127 by monks of the Order of Savigny, Furness later joined the Cistercians and became one of the richest abbeys in the land. Although the area became known as the Vale

of Deadly Nightshade because of the profusion of those plants, the Abbey's extensive remains, on a 73-acre (30-hectare) site, are breathtaking. Rose-red sandstone sits well against the green of well-manicured lawns.

The Dock Museum

Close by, on a loop in the railway line, is **Barrow-in-Furness**, a shipbuilding town with an impressive **Dock Museum** ❾ (www.dockmuseum. org.uk; Wed–Sun 11am–4pm, last admission 3.30pm; free). In a modern building built over an original Victorian dry dock, it has displays on geology, history, the influence of the Vikings and shipbuilding – Barrow remains the principal shipyard for producing Britain's submarines.

BROUGHTON AND MILLOM

From Barrow the railway turns north, with Duddon estuary gleaming to the west. Around the estuary, not far from the station at Foxfield, is **Broughton in Furness** (bus No. 7 from Foxfield; limited Mon–Sat service only). By car, take the A590 northwards and turn left onto the A595. Broughton is Old English and means a 'farmstead' or 'village by a stream'. The town has a market square, fine buildings, shady trees and a set of stocks once used to bring shame to felons.

The railway and road carry on around the side of the estuary and goose-frequented marshes, beneath brooding **Black Combe**, to reach the quaint Victorian town of **Millom**. You can also take bus No. 7

Xxxxxx

from Broughton to Millom (limited Mon–Sat service only). A beneficiary of the Furness ironstone boom, it was also the home of Norman Nicholson (1914–87), a poet in the Wordsworthian tradition deemed important enough to warrant a section in the **Discovery Centre** (www.millomdiscoverycentre.co.uk; Mon–Sat 10.30am–3.30pm, Sun 10.30am–1.30pm).

Less than a mile from the town of Millom on the A5093 are **Millom Castle** (a privately owned pele tower) and a restored 13th-century **church** that makes the area seem as if industrialisation passed it by.

DUDDON VALLEY

Sadly, there is no bus service north along the Duddon Valley. By car leave the A595 at Duddon Bridge, turning north to enter the **Duddon Valley** ❿. The road runs high, offering views across wooded hills, which in the days of Furness Abbey provided timber for charcoal and, in the 18th century,

supplied fuel for a **forge**, not far from Duddon Bridge, much of which is preserved. The iron ore was brought up the Duddon, and the forge had a ready charcoal supply. Wordsworth wrote a sequence of 35 sonnets about the River Duddon, describing it as 'majestic' and, at Duddon Bridge, making 'radiant progress towards the deep'. You can take bus No.7 (limited Mon–Sat service) as far as Duddon Bridge but no bus goes further north. There are some good walks from the bridge.

The Duddon frolics between jumbled boulders and bracken fronds, providing perfect picnic areas, though being secluded, the valley does not attract a great many visitors. Humans have lived in these parts for several thousand years, as witnessed by sepulchral mounds on the nearby hills in which calcified bones have been found.

Birks Bridge

The most attractive part of Duddon Valley is where **Birks Bridge**, a single span over a gorge, enables people

Taking a well-earned rest in the hills above Duddon Valley.

Old stone bridge over the River Duddon.

Norse name is derived from 'clearing of the shieling', a summer pasture, and it is not to be confused with Seathwaite in Borrowdale. Wordsworth stayed at its 16th-century Newfield Inn, which is still popular with walkers.

One of the poet's Duddon Sonnets is dedicated to Robert Walker, who was curate at Seathwaite for well over 60 years. Wordsworth called him 'Wonderful' Walker because of his good deeds and charity. As parson he performed many functions: outside is a stone that he used when clipping sheep.

Nearby is the rather bleak Seathwaite Tarn, which was dammed in 1904 to supply water to the growing industrial towns on the coast. It was featured in Richard Adams' *Plague Dogs*.

to cross the swirling river. The pools have a dark green hue, and rowans have rooted among the rocks. The big conifer forest to the west of the river dates back 70 years, to when the Forestry Commission planted dense ranks of alien spruce. There are now picnic areas and other facilities for public use.

SEATHWAITE

The hamlet of **Seathwaite** ⑪ is the largest in the Duddon Valley. Its

From Seathwaite the road finally meets the Wrynose and Hardknott Passes (see page 92) at **Cockley Beck**, with a turn west for Eskdale and east for Ambleside. To continue the tour you need to retrace your steps back to Broughton-in-Furness and take the A595 and A5092 to Ulverston. You can take the No. 7 bus from Duddon Bridge to Dalton-in-Furness and either take the train, or bus 6/X6, back to Ulverston.

The Kirk of Ulpha

Ulpha, between Duddon Bridge and Seathwaite, has a pretty church – Wordsworth's 'Kirk of Ulpha' – perched on a knoll beside the road and dedicated to St John the Baptist. The font is ancient, and the altar is made from cherry wood. 'Ulf, son of Evard' gave his name to the settlement, when he received the estate following the 1066 Norman Conquest, and his descendants had it for some 200 years.

'...To the pilgrim's eyes, as welcome as a star,' wrote Wordsworth.

Grizedale Forest

There is no public transport to **Grizedale Forest ⑫** from Ulverston. The forest was developed on an 8,000-acre (3,237-hectare) estate purchased by the Forestry Commission in 1937 and is reached from Ulverston via the A590 northwards followed by a left turn. During World War II, Grizedale Hall, a 40-room mansion at the heart of the estate, was used to house prisoners and was known as 'U-Boat Hotel'. The outbuildings of the now-dismantled hall have been incorporated into the excellent Grizedale Visitor Centre.

After the war, the Commission planted a commercial forest to which the public is granted access in order to learn about the countryside and walk along waymarked paths, including eight marked paths of the **Grizedale Sculpture Trail**, with work by young artists. The visitor centre (www. forestry.gov.uk/grizedalehome; daily 10am–5pm, closes 4pm in winter) has bike hire and a café. Also within the forest is **Go Ape!** (www.goape.co.uk; tel: 033-331 7293; book in advance), a high-ropes aerial course that swings Tarzan-like through the tree tops; there's also the new Go Ape Forest Segway adventure.

Young cyclists riding in Grizedale Forest.

The railway, motor museum and aquarium

From Ulverston take bus Nos 6/X6 to Haverthwaite, where you can catch the **Lakeside and Haverthwaite Railway** up to the shores of Windermere (www.lakesiderailway. co.uk; daily Apr–Oct). The trains connect with the steamers that cross the lake to Bowness (see page 21). The branch line was taken over by volunteers in 1970 and it preserves a variety of handsome British steam and diesel engines.

Bleak Seathwaite Tarn may not be very photogenic, but from Seathwaite village a walk in the Duddon Valley will provide a more scenic walk.

The buses also stop near the **Lakeland Motor Museum** ⓭ (www.lakelandmotormuseum.co.uk; daily Apr–Oct 9.30am–5.30pm, Nov–Mar 9.30am–4.30pm) at Backbarrow, just south of Newby Bridge. In a purpose-built museum by the river, this collection consists of some 30,000 motoring-related exhibits, including classic cars, motorcycles and bicycles. The museum pays tribute to the father-and-son Campbell water-speed duo (see page 44), with replicas of their famous *Bluebird* racing machines.

At Lakeside is the highly entertaining **Lakes Aquarium** ⓮ (www.lakesaquarium.co.uk; daily 9am–6pm, closing times vary throughout the year, check the website), where you can take a walk, literally, through a re-created part of Windermere, explore the aquatic life of Morecambe Bay and see the otters, baby crocodiles and cute marmosets.

Eating Out

Cartmel

The Cavendish Arms
Cavendish Street; www.thecavendisharms.co.uk; tel: 015395-36240; Mon–Sat noon–2pm, 6–9.30pm, Sun noon–9.30pm.
This hotel restaurant is a cut above the average, with excellent main courses of locally reared meat and tasty baps for lunch. ££

L'Enclume
Cavendish Street; www.lenclume.co.uk; tel: 015395-36362; daily 6.30–9pm, Tue–Sun noon–1.30pm.
With two Michelin stars this restaurant is certainly the most inventive, if not the best, in the Lakes. Run by chef Simon Rogan, the food is an intriguing mix of traditional and modern, making great use of a range of ingredients foraged from the wild. £££

Holker

The Cavendish Room
Holker Hall; www.holker.co.uk; tel: 015395-58328; Apr–Oct Wed–Sun 10.30am–5pm.
The food in the café at Holker Hall draws on the estate's top-notch produce; don't miss out on the superb home-made ice cream. ££

Ulverston

The Farmers Arms
Market Place; www.thefarmersulverston.co.uk; tel: 01229-584469; daily 11.30am–3pm, 5pm–8.30pm.
This traditional pub in the centre of town, also serves breakfast at 9am. Good ales and home-cooked food, including seafood specials. ££

Broughton in Furness

The Blacksmith's Arms
Broughton Mills; www.theblacksmithsarms.com; tel: 01229-716824; summer Mon 5–11pm, Tue–Sun noon–11pm, winter Mon 5–11pm, Tue–Fri noon–2.30pm and 5–11pm, Sat noon–11pm, Sun noon–10.30pm.
This cosy traditional pub has a good range of local beers, as well as tasty food, including Herdwick lamb and some good vegetarian options. ££

Haverthwaite

Station Restaurant
Lakeside and Haverthwaite Railway; www.lakesiderailway.co.uk; tel: 015395-31594; Apr–Oct daily 9am–5pm (last orders 4pm).
For those with a big appetite the hearty Railwayman's breakfast and the huge scones for afternoon tea will leave you satisfied. There are light bites and soups also available. £

Rowing boats on the shore of Derwent Water.

Pony trekking is a fun way to discover the Lakes.

Travel Tips

Active Pursuits

Variations on the 'activity' theme in an area of mountains, crags and lakes are limitless. Information is available from the Tourist Board (www.golakes.co.uk), by visiting the website of the National Park (www.lake-district.gov.uk) or www.ntlakesoutdoors.org.uk. The National Park and Tourist Board have a very useful range of leaflets– on walking, cycle routes and other activities – that can be downloaded from their websites.

WALKING

The most common form of recreation in the Lake District is walking, and the shelves of Lake District bookshops are crammed with guide books, most of which describe walking circular routes, of which the best and most evocative are the Wainwright Pictorial Guides (see box). The Ordnance Survey maps, especially the 1:25,000 series, are very detailed, perhaps too much for most uses. The waterproof and tough Harvey Maps, specially made for walking, climbing and cycling, are extremely good and very legible at a scale of 1:40,000. Their Lake District British Mountain Map is perhaps the best of any available, as one single sheet covers all the major fells.

The Lake District National Park organises walks for visitors, a full calendar being given on their website. Information Centres stock local maps showing walks suitable for people with disabilities.

A good short walk (about 2½ hours) is round Buttermere, one of the quieter lakes, starting at a car park in the village. Somewhat longer is the circumnavigation of Grasmere and Rydal, beginning at one of the car parks of Grasmere and walking on a well-beaten path to the west of the lakes, one stretch of the way being the celebrated Loughrigg Terrace. Re-

Alfred Wainwright

The best-known handbooks for walkers in the Lakes are the Pictorial Guides of Alfred Wainwright (1907–91). The original editions are now over 50 years old, but a second edition of each book, prepared by Chris Jesty, has retained their charm and brought the series up to date. A podcast giving fans a chance to 'walk with Wainwright' on Helm Crag can be found at www.golakes. co.uk/downloads.

Alfred Wainwright.

turn to Grasmere on a hillside path, which begins near Rydal Mount (see page 60).

Among the popular but more exacting hill walks of the Lake District is a circuit taking in the Langdale Pikes (see page 89), beginning and ending at the Dungeon Ghyll car park at the head of Great Langdale. In the east of the region, the summit of Helvellyn can be approached from either Thirlmere or Ullswater, a possible route from the latter being up the magnificent Striding Edge (see page 33).

In Central Lakeland, Great Gable can be ascended from Honister Pass, from Styhead Tarn at the head of Borrowdale, or from Wasdale Head. Wasdale Head is the most popular departure point for those wishing to conquer Scafell Pike. The southern fells are dominated by Coniston Old Man, and Skiddaw looms over the north.

CYCLING

One of the most popular ways to get around, and one that is being promoted heavily in the National Park, is by bike. Initially the Lakes might seem a challenging place for cyclists, and for some that is part of the appeal. For those who prefer an easier life, remember that rides around the lake shores or along the coast are quite flat and easy, and certain bus services (as well as the railway) will carry your bike, especially those of the Cross Lakes Experience.

The Tourist Information Offices have information on cycling routes, and you can download routes on www.go lakes.co.uk. Also check www.cycling cumbria.co.uk or www.mountain-bike-cumbria.co.uk. A number of routes lead around or through the Lakes, including the Coast to Coast ride (www. c2c-guide.co.uk). Those who are especially keen and fit might like to take up the Fred Whitton Challenge (www.

Cycling routes range from gentle, lakeside paths to off-road areas.

fredwhittonchallenge.org.uk), a 112-mile (180km) ride that takes in all the major passes in one day.

As well as road cycling, the Lake District is one of the best off-road cycling areas in the country. It is possible to hire mountain bikes in Ambleside, Coniston, Grizedale, Kendal, Keswick and Windermere. The Electric Bike Network (www.electricbicyclenetwork.com) lets the bike take the strain. Check the website for routes and hire points.

WATER SPORTS

Water sports are well catered for around Windermere, including windsurfing and water-skiing. Because of new speed restrictions (10mph/16kph) on power boats, some water sports are not permissible.

Swimming

While there are a handful of indoor swimming pools in the Lake District (in Keswick and Cockermouth, www.allerdale.gov.uk and in Penrith, Ulverston and Kendal, www.northcountryleisure.org.uk), the real joy of

> ## Pony and Llama Trekking
>
> This is a great activity for children, with the ponies following the green tracks, previously used to move goods from one settlement to another and to carry wool into Kendal (Lakeland Pony Treks; www.lakelandponytreks.co.uk). Equally enjoyable, and a little different, are Lakeland Llama Treks (www.lakelandllamatreks.co.uk).

swimming in the Lakes is outdoors in natural bodies of water. Some of the best places, with excellent water quality, are given below. However, do be aware that the water will be cold, especially in the deeper or higher lakes, so you will become tired more quickly than usual. In general it is best to stick to the shore, well out of the way of any boats and where the water is likely to be shallower and warmer. See also www.wildswimming.co.uk for some more unusual dips.

Windermere and Coniston Water are both used for outdoor swimming,

Swimming event on Lake Windermere.

For children not up for long walks, pony trekking is a great alternative.

and Windermere is the site for the annual 1-mile (1.5km) Great North Swim (see www.greatrun.org/greatswim for information). Millerground near Bowness on Windermere is a popular spot, as is Red Nab (though less busy). On Coniston, there are many places along the eastern shore, though on both lakes do keep an eye open for boats.

Ullswater is a shallow and safe place to swim, as are the smaller lakes of Rydal Water, Crummock Water and Buttermere. In Borrowdale the pools along Langstrath Beck provide some delightful swimming holes.

Sailing and kayaking

The Lakes are Arthur Ransome (author of the *Swallows and Amazons* series of children's books) country, and in the minds of many people irrevocably linked to sailing. The Lakes can be an excellent place to learn to sail, such as the Ark Sailing School Royal Yachting Association dinghy sailing course (www.arksailing.co.uk) on Windermere. As the largest of the lakes, Windermere is the major centre for sailing, and a number of other companies also offer courses or boat hire on the lake. Try River Deep Mountain High (www.riverdeepmountainhigh.co.uk) or Out-

run Sailing (www.outrunsailing.co.uk). There are also RYA courses and boats for hire on Ullswater (www.glenriddingsailingcentre.co.uk) and Derwent Water (www.derwentwatermarina.co.uk). Run by the National Park, the Coniston Boating Centre (www.conistonboatingcentre.co.uk) hires out sailing dinghies, kayaks and electrically driven motor boats.

There is both excellent white-water and sea kayaking on offer. For infor-

Kayaking on Ullswater, where you'll also find boats for hire.

With children, it is best to keep to the safe, supervised structures like the ones at the Lakeland Climbing Centre (www.kendalwall.co.uk).

mation on rivers, sea conditions and access check out www.canoe-england-cumbria.org.uk.

CLIMBING

Although there is a wide range of climbs in the Lake District, this is not a sport that can be undertaken casually. Many people learn through one of the specialist guides working in the Lakes. Wasdale is a favourite of many an experienced climber, and Langdale, Coniston and Pillar rocks are durable and popular. Climbers might be seen on crags near the Jaws of Borrowdale, and there are some nursery pitches not far from the Bowder Stone. This is also classic bouldering territory, and there are almost unlimited possibilities for this in the region (see www.lakesbloc.com for a list of areas and challenging climbs).

Shops selling outdoor garb usually have a stock of climbing books: try Rock and Run (www.rockrun.com) in Ambleside or Needle Sports (www.needlesports.com) in Keswick.

More information on climbing can be had from the British Mountaineering Council (www.thebmc.co.uk).

FELL RUNNING

A particularly gruelling form of Lakeland outdoor activity, fell running is exactly what it seems, racing long distances over the hills. Perhaps the greatest of all runners is the legendary Joss Naylor, a Cumbrian sheep farmer, who set and broke many records. Races are held regularly throughout the season, and much information can be found on the Fell Runners' Association website (www.fellrunner.org.uk).

The most famous challenge for fell runners is the Bob Graham Round, covering 66 miles (106km), 27,000ft (8,2390m) and 42 of the highest peaks, all within 24 hours (see www.bobgrahamclub.co.uk for more information). If you are interested in seeing – or following – the actual routes, Harvey have a large number of maps covering each of the major races.

Themed Holidays

The Lake District region naturally lends itself to a variety of outdoor holidays, from walking to cycling to sailing. However, there are many other ways to structure your holiday in the Lakes, from cookery and relaxing at a spa, to birdwatching and literary pilgrimages.

CHILDREN

Facilities for children range from theme attractions, such as those associated with Beatrix Potter (in both Hawkshead and Bowness) and parks, such as Grizedale Forest, to adventurous activities including camping and canoeing, as written about so evocatively in the 1930s and '40s by Arthur Ransome in the adventures of the *Swallows and Amazons* (expert tuition is available in most areas). A number of places have adventure playgrounds, one of the best being at Brockhole Visitor Centre (see page 35). In general, however, children will tend to enjoy the same attractions in the Lakes – the water, fells and wildlife – as adults, making a good all-round destination for families.

COOKING

The Lake District has become something of a foodie destination in recent years, and there are a number of excellent cookery courses you can attend. A good range of day courses (3–7 hours), from breadmaking to seafood preparation, can be found at the Peter Sidwell Cookery School (www.rheged.com). Also well worth checking out are Lucy Cooks (www.lucycooks.co.uk), with courses for both children and adults, and, if you want to explore local foods, Cumbria on a Plate (www.cumbriaonaplate.co.uk).

LITERARY TOURS

Many visitors are drawn to the Lakes through their love of the works of a particular writer. This could involve sites associated with William Wordsworth or John Ruskin, or – also of interest to children – tracking down the sites that inspired Beatrix Potter or Arthur Ransome. Richardson and Gray (www.richardsonandgray.com) is a specialist operator, which can arrange tours of literary sites; otherwise contact Cumbria Tourist Guides (www.cumbriatouristguides.co.uk).

NATURE- AND BIRDWATCHING

Between red deer and red squirrels, there is great scope for a nature-based holiday in the Lakes (see www.cumbriawildlifetrust.org.uk for more information and the feature on page 86). The diverse Lakeland environment also hosts a wide range of birdlife. Buzzards, ravens and peregrines inhabit the higher elevations throughout the year, while numer-

Literary buffs should visit John Ruskin's home at Brantwood.

ous species of waterfowl populate the freshwater lagoons, salt marshes and mudflats. Spring is the best time to spot migratory species in the lower woodland slopes and valleys. Wild ospreys have returned to England and can be seen near Bassenthwaite Lake (see page 83).

Geology

The Lake District's complex and fascinating geology can form the basis for your holiday, either on a purpose-run course like those run by HF Holidays (www.hfholidays.co.uk), or organised by yourself. The British Geological Survey publishes a *Lake District Geology Holiday Map* to help you identify the different rocks of the area. Visits to mines will also help you understand the underlying structure of the Lakes, and the economic importance of the minerals to be found there. The three mines open to visitors are: Haig Pit Mining and Colliery Museum (www.haig-pit.co.uk); Honister Slate Mine (www.honister.com); and Threlkeld Quarry

Mining Museum (www.threlkeldquarry andminingmuseum.co.uk).

SPAS

A spa break may not be the first thing that springs to mind in the Lakes, but there are a number of excellent places to unwind and have treatments. These, coupled with the beautiful landscape and good food, make for a truly relaxing escape. Of the hotel spas, those at Armathwaite Hall (www.armathwaite-hall.com) and Lakeside Hotel (www.lakesidehotel.co.uk) are particularly good. For day spas check out Oxley's (www.oxleyshealthspa.co.uk) in Ambleside.

VOLUNTEERING

A constructive way of spending your holiday might be to volunteer with an organisation that conserves or protects the environment of the Lake District. The Fix the Fells programme (www.fixthefells.co.uk) looks after and repairs the heavily used footpaths on the mountains, while Friends of the

The Spa at Armathwaite Hall offers, free to residents, the choice of physical exercise or relaxation, as the mood dictates.

Lake District (www.friendsofthelake district.org.uk) run a number of conservation programmes. If you are interested in wildlife protection contact the Cumbria Wildlife Trust (www.cumbriawildlifetrust.org.uk).

WALKING, CYCLING AND SAILING

Outdoor activities take pride of place in the Lakes, and many companies run guided walks, tours or rides. See page 112 for details of day walks and cycle routes. Walkabout Holidays (www.walkaboutholidays.com) offer a wide range of guided day and multi-day walks in the Lakes. For 2–14 day walking packages try Lake District Guided Walking (www.lakedistrict guidedwalking.co.uk).

Although you can, of course, plan your own cycle rides, there are a number of companies providing supported and guided multi-day rides around the Lakes, including CycleActive (www.cycleactive.com).

A holiday can also be built around working towards an RYA (Royal Yachting Association; www.rya.org. uk) qualification. See the websites under *Active Pursuits*, page 112.

Feeding the birds on Windermere, where sailing is popular.

The Lakes by Rail

The Lake District's two preserved railways make excellent days out for children: the Ravenglass and Eskdale Railway (www.ravenglass-railway.co.uk) runs from Ravenglass to Dalegarth, while the Lakeside and Haverthwaite Railway (www.lakeside railway.co.uk) runs south from the southern end of Windermere.

The Ravenglass and Eskdale Railway has a discounted travel pass for visitors staying a few days in the area, or intending to travel several times in the year.

Practical Information

GETTING THERE

By train

Virgin trains from London to Oxen-holme (connecting with a local service to Windermere) take less than 3 hours, and from Edinburgh to Carlisle 1.5 hours, a little longer to Penrith. From Yorkshire the spectacular Settle–Carlisle railway is served by Northern Rail. Northern Rail also runs the scenic Cumbria Coast Line connecting Barrow-in-Furness, Whitehaven and Carlisle. The Furness Line from Lancaster connects Grange-over-Sands, Cartmel and Barrow-in-Furness. Details of all rail services are available from National Rail Enquiries (www.nationalrail.co.uk).

By coach

National Express runs the Express Rapide service from London (Victoria) to Kendal. For details of this and other coach services to the area see www.nationalexpress.com.

Be extra careful when driving in the area, as the roads are often quite challenging.

By road

The Lake District is about 5½ hours from London by road. The M6 gives quick access to the Lake District, with exits at Lancaster, the Kendal bypass, Shap and Penrith. By road from Dover to Windermere is 353 miles (570km); from the North Sea ferry at Hull to Windermere is 139 miles (224km).

By air

Many overseas visitors find Manchester Airport most convenient for Cumbria. Manchester is adjacent to the M6, which runs along the eastern fringe of the Lake District. Trains depart from the airport railway station to Barrow-in-Furness, Windermere, Penrith and Carlisle. Liverpool John Lennon, Leeds/Bradford, Newcastle and Blackpool airports are also within striking distance.

GETTING AROUND

For details of bus and rail services throughout Cumbria, contact Traveline (tel: 0871-200 2233; www.travel ine.org.uk) or consult the nearest Tourist Information Centre (see page 123). Public transport information can be downloaded (www.cumbria. gov.uk; www.golakes.co.uk) or found in tourist information offices and libraries. Special-offer combined bus and boat tickets can be used for boats on Windermere and Stagecoach North West buses.

By bus

Details of the Lake District's extensive bus services are given in the routes in this book. It is important to note that routes and timetables may be changed at short notice. The company operating the largest number of routes is Stagecoach (www.stagcoachbus.com).

Several smaller bus companies run services, many of which are seasonal. Other useful websites are Mountain Goat tours and services, www.mountain-goat.co.uk, who also operate the Cross Lakes Experience (Apr–Oct); and the Cumbria tourist information site, www.golakes.com/travel. See also www.cumbria.gov.uk\buses.

By train

The 72-mile (116km) Settle–Carlisle line travels through the north–south valleys of the Ribble and Eden between the Lakeland fells and the Pennines. Equally impressive is the stretch of track that takes in the Cumbrian coast, from Lancaster or Barrow-in-Furness to Carlisle. Starting from Lancaster allows a return from Carlisle to Lancaster over Shap Fell and through the Lune Gorge. The short branch line from Oxenholme on the main line will take you to the shores of Windermere. For all these services check National Rail Enquiries.

The Ravenglass and Eskdale Railway operates over 7 miles (11km) of track through Eskdale (tel: 01229-717171; www.ravenglass-railway.co.uk). The Lakeside and Haverthwaite Railway (tel: 015395-31594; www.lakeside railway.co.uk) connects at Lakeside, Windermere, with a 'steamer' voyage to Bowness and Waterhead.

By bike

Although the Lake District is very hilly and some of the cycling can be strenuous, this can be a very rewarding way of getting around, both on- and off-road (see page 113). The Electric Bike Network offers a less strenuous way of tackling the hills (www.electricbicyclenetwork.com).

By car

While travelling by car offers a very handy form of transport in the Lakes,

There are several ferries operating on Windermere.

at peak times it causes acute congestion, so where at all possible try to use public transport (details are given in all the routes) or get out into the beautiful countryside and explore by bike or on foot. If you do need to hire a car, local services include:

Enterprise, Station Road, Kendal; www.enterprise.co.uk.

Lakes Car Hire, New Road, Windermere; www.lakeshire.co.uk.

Practical, Ullswater Road, Penrith; www.practical.co.uk.

By boat

Regular boat services operate on several of the lakes, often connecting with the bus or train.

Coniston Water: Coniston Launch, Pier Cottage, Coniston; tel: 017687-75753; www.conistonlaunch.co.uk.

Derwent Water: Keswick Launch Company, 29 Manor Park, Keswick; tel: 017687-72263; www.keswick-launch.co.uk.

Ullswater: Ullswater Steamers, The Pier House, Glenridding; tel: 017684-82229; www.ullswater-steamers.co.uk.

Windermere: Windermere Lake Cruises, Pier 3, Bowness-on-Windermere; tel: 015394-43360; www.windermere-lakecruises.co.uk.

Guided tours

There are a number of companies offering guided minibus tours of the Lakes. The following are well established and have a good reputation:

Mountain Goat, Victoria Street, Windermere; tel: 015394-45161; www.mountain-goat.co.uk.

Lake District Tours, Fellside Cottage, Witherslack; tel: 015395-52106; www.lakedistricttours.co.uk.

Lakes Supertours, 1 High Street, Windermere; tel: 015394-42751; www.lakes-supertours.com.

FACTS FOR THE VISITOR

Disabled travellers

Access is improving all the time for disabled travellers to the Lakes, especially for those wishing to take part in outdoor activities. Wheelchairs can be hired at the Bowness-on-Windermere information centres. See the National Park website for information on the 42 Miles Without Stiles routes that are suitable for the visually impaired and wheelchair users. For general information contact or visit the National Park Visitor Centre (www.lake-district.gov.uk). Information on travel within the UK can be found on the Disabled Travel Advice website (www.disabledtraveladvice.co.uk) or www.direct.gov.uk.

Emergencies

For **police**, **ambulance**, **fire brigade** or **mountain rescue** tel: 999 or 112. Please do not call mountain rescue unless it is a true emergency; there have been reports of some walkers calling merely because they feel a bit tired.

Nationals of the European Union are entitled to free medical treatment in the UK. Some other countries also have reciprocal arrangements for free treatment. However, most visitors from abroad have to pay for medical and dental treatment and should ensure that they have adequate health insurance. Furness General Hospital in Barrow-in-Furness has a 24-hour accident and emergency unit, and Westmorland General Hospital in Kendal has an accident and minor emergency unit. For general health information

Mountain Rescue is to be called upon only in case of true emergencies.

and diagnosis over the telephone call the NHS (tel: 111). More information, including a list of local services, can be found on their website (www.nhs.uk).

Opening hours

Shops are usually open Mon–Sat 9 or 9.30am–5 or 5.30pm. In larger towns and more popular areas shops are likely to stay open later and on Sundays. Banks tend to open Mon–Fri 9am–5pm, though some major branches may also open on Saturday mornings. Tourist Offices are usually open daily 9.30am–5.30pm in the summer and 10am–4pm during the winter (some closed Sundays).

Tourist information

The Cumbria Tourist Board has a comprehensive network of tourist offices across the Lake District. The major ones are listed below; some have their own websites, and a great deal more useful information can be found on the main website (www. golakes.co.uk). The National Park Authority has a number of visitor centres across the district, the main one being the Lake District Visitor Centre at Brockhole, listed below, and their website (www.lake-district.gov.uk) is also good source of information.

Local and Cumbria Tourist Board Offices

Ambleside, Central Buildings, Market Cross; tel: 015394-32582; email: tic@thehubofambleside.com.

Coniston, Ruskin Avenue; tel: 015394-41533; www.conistontic.org.

Hawkshead, Main Street; tel: 015394-39646; www.hawksheadtouristinfo.org.uk.

Kendal, 25 Stramongate; tel: 01539-735891; email: info@kendaltic.co.uk.

Penrith, Penrith Museum, Middlegate; tel: 01768-867466; www.visiteden.co.uk.

Parking is hard to find in Bowness-on-Windermere.

Windermere, Victoria Street; tel: 015394-46499; www.windermereinfo.co.uk.

National Park Information Centres

Bowness, Glebe Road; tel: 0845-901 0845; email: BownessTIC@lakedistrict.gov.uk.

Brockhole, Windermere; tel: 015394-46601; www.brockhole.co.uk.

Keswick, Moot Hall, Market Square; tel: 0845-901 0845; email: KeswickTIC@lakedistrict.gov.uk.

Ullswater, Beckside Car Park, Glenridding; tel: 017684-82414; email: ullswatertic@lakedistrict.gov.uk.

Entertainment

There are a number of cinemas and theatres in Lakeland, including:

Ambleside: Zeffirellis (cinema), Compston Road; www.zeffirellis.com.

Kendal: The Brewery Arts Centre, Highgate; www.breweryarts.co.uk.

Keswick: Theatre by the Lake, Lakeside; www.theatrebythelake.com.

Penrith: The Playhouse, Auctionmart Lane; www.penrithplayers.co.uk; Rheged (cinema), Redhills; www.rheged.com.

Accommodation

In the Lake District accommodation ranges from basic youth hostels to luxurious country-house hotels, and, as befits one of the most popular areas of the country, there are a huge number of places to stay. Many hotels can be found around the major lakes, especially Windermere.

The price guide for the basic cost of a double room per night during high season is as follows:

£££ = over £180
££ = £110–180
£ = under £110

Because of the high demand, the Lake District is not especially cheap, and prices can rocket in high season. Breakfast is usually included in the price of the room.

Windermere and Bowness
The Cranleigh Boutique
Kendal Road, Bowness-on-Windermere; tel: 015394-43293; www.thecranleigh.com.

A stunningly designed hotel, where each of the 18 sumptuous rooms has a unique contemporary style, plus amazing bathrooms complete with indulgent facilities. New for 2015 are four opulent suites (£££). ££

The Hideaway
Phoenix Way, Windermere; tel: 015394-43070; www.thehideawayatwindermere.co.uk.

Built in 1890, this tasteful hotel still retains many of its Victorian features, and is a friendly, peaceful place to stay. Nicely low-key, the rooms are modern with great bathrooms. Tea and homemade cakes are included. ££

Linthwaite House Hotel
Crook Road, Windermere; tel: 015394-88600; www.linthwaite.com.

This is one of the best hotels in the Lake District, in a sublime hilltop setting overlooking Lake Windermere. Bedrooms are very stylish, and award-winning British food is served up in the restaurant. £££

Miller Howe
Rayrigg Road, Windermere; tel: 015394-42536; www.millerhowe.com.

Set in acres of landscaped gardens right on the lake shore, the hotel offers spacious, individually decorated

Some accommodations have a pub attached.

rooms, all with balconies and several with panoramic views. Dining is a treat looking out over the lake. ££

Crosthwaite
The Punch Bowl
Tel: 015395-68237; www.the-punch bowl.co.uk.
A historic inn nestled in the heart of the Lyth Valley. Full of character, the rooms have huge bathrooms with free-standing roll-top baths. Eat contemporary food in the formal restaurant or traditional pub food in the bar. Rooms are cheaper during the week. £££

Ullswater
Sharrow Bay
Tel: 01768-486301; www.sharrow bay.co.uk.
In a breathtaking lakeside setting, this long-established 'country-house hotel' is very traditional. The bedrooms ooze luxurious elegance, full of porcelain, pictures and antiques; the perfect tranquil retreat. £££

Ambleside and Rydal
Randy Pike
Outgate; tel: 015394-36088; www.randypike.co.uk.
Housed in a restored hunting lodge, where the original character is still most evident in the three chic suites with a quirky touch. Brought to you by the owners of the excellent Jumble Room restaurant in Grasmere. £££

Coniston
The Black Bull and Hotel
Tel: 015394-41335; www.blackbull coniston.co.uk.
This 400-year old coaching inn has nine rooms in the pub itself and six rooms separate from the main building, all well appointed. Good local food available and beer from their own microbrewery. £

Hawkshead and Sawrey
The Love Shack
Sawrey; tel: 015394-41242; www.lake districtloveshack.com.
Looking for a secluded retreat? Then this designer-cool hideaway in the woods, housed in a sustainably designed wooden building, is for you. There is a minimum three-days' stay, with organic food available if required. ££
Red Lion Inn
The Square, Hawkshead; tel: 015394 36213; www.redlionhawkshead.co.uk.
The rooms here are attractive, comfortable and set in a fine 15th-century coaching inn, which is popular with locals. A good bet in the budget range. £

Keswick
Greta Hall
Main Street; tel: 017687-75980; www.gretahall.net.
The former home of poets Coleridge and Southey is available for extremely comfortable self-catering lets; there is also one en-suite bed-and-breakfast room. The attractively austere rooms are well equipped, and the owners pride themselves on their green credentials. ££

Borrowdale
Hazel Bank Country House
Rosthwaite; tel: 017687-77248; www.hazelbankhotel.co.uk.
A traditional Lakeland stone, 19th-century building set in its own wooded grounds with atmospheric, well-preserved rooms and a super friendly welcome. The AA Rosette awarded restaurant overlooks the garden with a vista of local wildlife. £
Seatoller House
Seatoller; tel: 017687-77218; www.seatollerhouse.co.uk.
Ten pretty, comfortable guest rooms are found within this attractive stone house standing at the head of Bor-

rowdale Lake. The guest house prides itself on tasty local food and a friendly welcome; it makes a good base for walkers and painters. £

Cockermouth
The Allerdale Court Hotel
Market Place; tel: 01900-823654; www.allerdalecourthotel.co.uk.
The spacious guest rooms in this 17th-century house are said to have been used by HMS *Bounty* mutineer Fletcher Christian. Open log fires and oak beams set the scene, blending perfectly with modern style. £

Bassenthwaite
Armathwaite Hall
Bassenthwaite Lake; tel: 017687-76551; www.armathwaite-hall.com.
Luxurious accommodation in an imposing stately house surrounded by magnificent grounds; each room has different features from rooftop terrace to spa baths. But the real pull is the excellent spa. £££
The Cottage in the Wood
Whinlatter Pass, Braithwaite; tel: 017687-78409; www.thecottageinthe wood.co.uk.
Tucked away in a beautiful mountainous location, this former 17th-century coaching inn has delightfully stylish rooms and a fine restaurant that supports quality local suppliers. Very peaceful, yet only 5 miles (8km) from bustling Keswick. ££

Langdale
Old Dungeon Ghyll Hotel
Tel: 015394-37272; www.odg.co.uk.
A climbers' retreat that offers well-priced, pretty rooms and decent food. The comfortable lounge, complete with open fire, provides an ideal place to relax after a strenuous day in the mountains enjoying breathtaking scenery. ££

Cartmel
Aynsome Manor Hotel
Aynsome Lane; tel: 015395-36653; www.aynsomemanorhotel.co.uk.
Two generations of the same family have created a warm country-house feel throughout this 16th-century manor. Some of the smart rooms are built around a courtyard, while two are housed in a separate converted 16th-century stable block. ££
L'Enclume
Cavendish Street; tel: 015395-36362; www.lenclume.co.uk.
This restaurant boasting two Michelin stars has one of the country's most innovative chefs, Simon Rogan, at the helm. Although the food takes centre stage, the 12 individually designed guest rooms are elegant, modern and very nice indeed. ££

Newby Bridge
Swan Hotel & Spa
Tel: 015395-31681; www.swanhotel.com.
Inside this 17th-century coaching inn is a modern, chic and family-friendly hotel. Standing at the southern tip of Lake Windermere, this grand old building conceals bright attractive bedrooms, a first-class restaurant, spa and tremendous views all around. ££

ACCOMMODATION WEBSITES

Go Lakes has a huge selection of places to stay and straightforward online booking: www.golakes.co.uk. The **Landmark Trust** has a number of historic self-catering properties: www.landmarktrust.org.uk. The **YHA** (Youth Hostel Association) has an excellent network of places to stay: www.yha.org.uk. An alternative to the youth hostels is **Camping Barns**: www.lakelandcampingbarns.co.uk.

Index

Credits

Insight Guides Great Breaks Lake District
Editor: Rachel Lawrence
Authors: Alyse Dar, Maria Lord, W.R. Mitchell
Head of Production: Rebeka Davies
Picture Editor: Tom Smyth
Cartography Update: Carte
Photo credits: A Brief Moment in Time 119B; Alamy 20B, 22T, 22B, 23B, 24B, 24T, 37B, 73T, 81B, 93B, 122; Alan Cleaver 57B, 72T, 76; Armathwaite Hall 118; Cumbria Photo/Andrew Lugsen 74T; Cumbria Photo/Ben Barden 6ML, 46T, 51, 66, 69T, 80B, 113B, 117; Cumbria Photo/Brian Sherwen 32T, 79, 93T; Cumbria Photo/Dave Willis 21, 31T, 37T, 46B, 48T, 50B, 55B, 59B, 60T, 68T, 80T, 83, 88, 94T, 111, 112, 115T; Cumbria Photo/Steve Barber 12, 35T, 64ML, 65T, 116; Cumbria Photo/Tony West 11T, 16B, 18B, 18T, 35, 38T, 43, 54, 55T, 67, 68B, 89T, 91, 106, 108T, 119T; Flickr/clurr 69B; Flickr/ Duncanh1 40ML; Flickr/johndal 71T; Getty Images 4/5, 8/9, 49B, 84B, 86TL, 87T, 90, 95B, 101T, 102T, 108B, 124; Holker Hall 100B, 101B; iStock 6MC, 7TR, 7M, 10B, 14, 19T, 27, 30T, 45, 48B, 52, 53, 56B, 56T, 62T, 63, 70B, 71, 73B, 74B, 75, 77T, 84T, 85, 86ML, 95, 103B, 105, 107B, 107T; Lyth Damson 13; Mike Lawrence 83; NTPL/Nadia Mackenzie 81T; Press Association Images 113T; Piddy77 7M; Public domain 6MR, 29B, 103T; Shutterstock 31B, 78, 89B, 96T, 96B, 114; Simon Collison 72B; William Shaw/Apa Publications 6ML, 7T, 7MR, 7BR, 9, 10T, 11B, 15, 16T, 17B, 17T, 19B, 21T, 23T, 26, 28, 29T, 30B, 32B, 33B, 33T, 34B, 36, 38B, 39, 40TL, 41T, 42, 45T, 44B, 47T, 47B, 49T, 50T, 57T, 58, 60B, 61B, 62B, 64TL, 77B, 92, 98, 100T, 102B, 105, 115B, 120, 121, 123; Wordsworth Trust 59T, 61T
Cover credits: Shutterstock (main and BL) iStock (BR)
No part of this book may be reproduced, stored in a retrieval system or transmitted in any form or means electronic, mechanical, photocopying, recording or otherwise, without prior written permission from APA Publications.

CONTACTING THE EDITORS:
Every effort has been made to provide accurate information in this publication, but changes are inevitable. The publisher cannot be responsible for any resulting loss, inconvenience or injury. We would appreciate it if readers would call our attention to any errors or outdated information. We also welcome your suggestions; please contact us at: hello@insightguides.com

Information has been obtained from sources believed to be reliable, but its accuracy and completeness, and the opinions based thereon, are not guaranteed.

All Rights Reserved
© 2016 Apa Digital (CH) AG and Apa Publications (UK) Ltd

Third Edition 2016

Printed in China by CTPS

Worldwide distribution enquiries:
APA Publications (Singapore) Pte, 7030 Ang Mo Kio Avenue 5, 08-65 Northstar @ AMK, Singapore 569880
apasin@signet.com.sg
Distributed in the UK and Ireland by:
Dorling Kindersley Ltd, A Penguin Group company, 80 Strand, London, WC2R 0RL
sales@uk.dk.com
Distributed in the US by:
Ingram Publisher Services, 1 Ingram Boulevard, PO Box 3006, La Vergne, TN 37086-1986
ips@ingramcontent.com
Distributed in Australia and New Zealand by:
Woodslane, 10 Apollo St, Warriewood, NSW 2102, Australia
info@woodslane.com.au